Anatomy

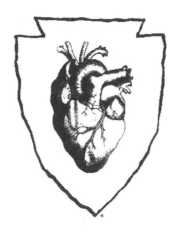

The 7 Virtues All Warriors Must Live by to

Successfully Protect and Serve

By

Alexander Lanshe

Anatomy of a Warrior

To Chelsea,

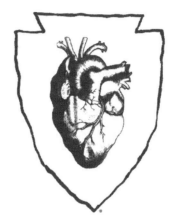

1/4/2020

Live with Virtue!

Alex Lawshe

PUBLISHED BY: Alexander Lanshe LLC - 1st Edition

DISCLAIMER AND/OR LEGAL NOTICES

While all attempts have been made to verify information provided in this

book and its ancillary materials, neither the author nor publisher assumes

any responsibility for errors, inaccuracies, or omissions and is not

responsible for any financial loss by customer in any manner. Any slights

of people or organizations are unintentional. If advice concerning legal,

financial, accounting or related matters is needed, the services of a

qualified professional should be sought. This book and its associated

ancillary materials, including verbal and written training, is not intended for

use as a source of legal, financial or accounting advice. You should be

aware of the various laws governing business transactions or other

business practices in your particular geographical location.

Unless specifically stated, the opinion, beliefs, content and worldview

expressed in this book is solely that of the author and should not be attributed to any particular one or group of the interviewees listed in the back of the book.

EARNINGS, INCOME & RESULTS DISCLAIMER

With respect to the reliability, accuracy, timeliness, usefulness, adequacy, completeness and/or suitability of information provided in this book, Alexander Lanshe, Alexander Lanshe LLC, its partners, associates, affiliates, consultants, and/or presenters make no warranties, guarantees, representations, or claims of any kind. Readers' results will vary depending on a number of factors. Testimonials are not representative. This book and all products and services are for educational and informational purposes only. You agree that Alexander Lanshe and/or Alexander Lanshe LLC is not responsible for the success or failure of your personal, business, health or financial decisions relating to any information presented by Alexander Lanshe, Alexander Lanshe LLC, or company products/services. Your, and all human potential, is entirely dependent on the efforts, skills and applications of the individual person.

Any examples, stories, references, or case studies are for illustrative purposes only and should not be interpreted as testimonials and/or examples of what reader and/or consumers can generally expect from the information. No representation in any part of this information, materials and/or seminar training are guarantees or promises for actual performance. Any statements, strategies, concepts, techniques, exercises, and ideas in the information, materials and/or seminar training offered are simply opinion or experience, and thus should not be misinterpreted as promises, typical results or guarantees (expressed or implied). The author and publisher (Alexander Lanshe, Alexander Lanshe LLC (ALLLC) or any of ALLLC's representatives) shall in no way, under any circumstances, be held liable to any party (or third party) for any direct, indirect, punitive, special, incidental or other consequential damages arising directly or indirectly from any use of books, materials and/or seminar trainings, which is provided "as is" and without warranties.

Table of Contents

Meaning of the Logo and Title of the Book

I believe that the true anatomy of a warrior is the content of your heart. The anatomical heart was chosen to symbolize this. Each warrior has a real, beating heart. If we could dissect this heart to see what virtues lay inside, we would discover the true anatomy of the warrior. This virtuous anatomy is what is valuable and beneficial to the world. The true anatomy of a warrior is not the physical flesh and bone but the seven core virtues of the heart.

The logo is an arrowhead (which also resembles a shield) surrounding an anatomical heart. The shield element communicates protection, a safe place, and a warrior. The shield is jagged and rough around the edges to symbolize human imperfection. Despite our imperfection, we take up our shield and our weapons and we fight on because it is our duty. Warriors use shields to protect themselves, their comrades and their nation. If you look at a shield, it communicates that behind it is a safe place - protection.

An arrowhead communicates speed, depth, penetration (or piercing) and is a lethal weapon that has been used for millennia to protect people. Like the arrow, you are a virtuous weapon of truth and righteousness capable of neutralizing conflict and violence.

The heart is anatomically correct because the shield is protecting real people - your heart and the hearts of others. The heart is anatomically correct to remind you of the reality and consequences of failing to protect. Real lives are at stake. The best thing you can do for yourself is to protect your own heart so that it may protect others. The shield around the heart reminds you of this.

Virtue is said to reside in and proceed from the heart. The virtue that you forge inside your heart is the true measure of whether or not you are a warrior. You make your heart safe from evil by living virtuously. The virtue that flows from your heart gives life and purpose to the weapons you take up (the shield and arrowhead) and reminds you why you fight. Virtue forges your character which hardens you against evil, weakness, and vice. If your own heart is not made safe how can you protect others? I believe that your goal should be to forge these virtues into the essence of your being so that you can live, serve and die as a warrior and a protector.

Affiliated Charities

Alex Lanshe has partnered with and chosen two charities to support. One for military veterans and one for Police Officers.

1. The Battle Continues (TBC)

Founded by interviewee and retired Army Captain, Dr. Sudip Bose, TBC "raises awareness about the struggles veterans go through upon return from the war. Our Board of Directors will allocate donated funds to veterans and their families to help them fight their battles which continue after combat."

- "100% of your donation goes directly to support a veteran or their families." – Dr. Sudip Bose

Here is their website where you can make an additional donation: http://thebattlecontinues.org/

2. Concerns of Police Survivors (C.O.P.S.)

"C.O.P.S. knows that a survivor's level of distress is directly affected by the agency's response to the tragedy. C.O.P.S., therefore, offers training and assistance to law enforcement agencies nationwide on how to respond to the tragic loss of a member of the law enforcement profession. C.O.P.S. programs and services are funded by grants and donations." Here is their website where you can make an additional donation: https://www.nationalcops.org/

Alex Lanshe's Top Tier Members & Clients

Special Gratitude & Recognition for Supreme Loyalty and Dedication

This book would not be possible without the special dedication, loyalty and support from these individuals. Pictured from L to R (all standing): Margaret Lanshe (my sister and sketch artist for the front cover logo), Randall Traub (3 Year Top Tier Client, lawyer who helped to trademark the logo & good friend), Candace Pryor (1 year Top Tier Client & friend), Lawrence Halmasy (4 year Top Tier Client

& good friend) and Adam McLaughlin (3 year Top Tier Client,

mentee and good friend). As my Top Tier Clients, you all provided

me with the support and financial freedom to focus on your training

and this book. Without your support I would not have had the

freedom to interview these 120 protectors nor been able to focus

exclusively on writing and completing this book. You all stuck with

me through hard times and have shown prolonged loyalty and

dedication to what we are building. I can never repay you for all your

kindness and loyalty. I thank you all from the bottom of my heart and

I look forward to our continued friendship as the years go on.

Live with Virtue!

Acknowledgments

First and foremost I am grateful to Almighty God, the blessed Trinity, for giving me the grace, strength, and fortitude to persevere with this project. He is my ultimate source and I believe Him to be the origin of all virtue. I pray for the continued grace to teach and share the message of the warrior virtues. All the glory to God.

I want to give a tremendous, heart-felt thank you to all the protectors and warriors who were interviewed for this project! You can see all their names in the back of the book under the "Interviewee List". Suffice to say this project is nothing without all of your selfless contributions. I am forever grateful to each and every one of you!

A sincere and humble thank you to Lt. Col. Dave Grossman for being the first interviewee and for writing such an amazing Foreword! Your willingness to sit down with me opened up the doors to 119 other amazing men and women. When I asked you to write the Foreword you said that it was "like being asked to be the Godfather of my child", and that you accepted whole-heartedly. I will never forget your kindness and enthusiasm in helping me with this book. Rangers truly lead the way Dave! HOOAH!

A huge thank-you to Gavin de Becker for writing such a stellar Afterword to this book. Your willingness and eagerness to help me with this book and to further the warrior virtues is quite admirable and I can never thank you enough for how generous you have been with your time.

Special thank you to a friend and mentor, Virgil Klunder. It was in your home back in January of 2015 that you suggested I begin interviewing the experts and top protectors and that I should write a book based on those interviews. This process has taught me many life lessons, extended my network, honed my interviewing skills, allowed me to make new friends, and helped to clarify my business and life purpose. Thank you. I am forever grateful for the visit we had in 2015 and this project would not exist without your help and guidance.

I want to thank a friend and mentor, James Malinchak. You took me under your wing as a young college student and shared with me a great deal's worth of business advice when I was unable to pay you for it. I want to thank you for being the first person to make me believe I could write a book and be a speaker. Before I met you, I never thought of writing a book, much less multiple books. Before we met, I never thought about being a speaker. Now, due to your influence, I have written 2 books, co-authored another and speak about those topics across the country. Thank you for all your support and encouragement over the years James.

I want to thank my parents, John and Faith Lanshe, for believing in me and what I am doing. You have always been there for me, you have given me good advice, and I sincerely hope that this book makes you proud. I can never repay you for all you have done and continue to do for me. I am proud to be your son and I am grateful for all the sacrifices you have made for me and my siblings. I love you both from the bottom of my heart!

A special thank-you to my siblings: Gabrielle, Gus, Madeline, Bernadette, Margaret and Gerard. You all helped me during the process of writing by providing me with conversation, support and down-time between my work. Some of you reviewed the book for grammatical errors as well - thank you! I love you all and am grateful that God made me your older brother.

Thank you to Mr. Kerry Hornick for sharing your Dojo space with me and my clients. Your location has been a fantastic place to train and we are all most grateful for your kindness.

Big thank you to Bill Bowers. You did a very thorough and prompt job editing this book. Thank you for working so quickly and with my time constraints.

I would like to thank my Grandparents, John & Jean Lanshe and Judith Flohr. All of you have been such a positive influence on my life and I am grateful to God that I had the privilege of having such amazing grandparents. I love you Papa, Mema, and Gram.

I would like to give a special thank-you to my favorite University Professor and philosopher, Joseph LiVecchi. Your training and classes sharpened my philosophical skills and helped me to realize that I have a passion for writing, study, and philosophy. Thank you for your guidance and for being passionate about what you do and passing that onto me. Your influence on my life has extended far beyond the classroom and I still remember much of what you taught me as it had a profound and lasting effect on my character and mind. Gratias tibi.

A deep and sincere thank you to Dr. Michael Dunphy and all the Shinbukan seniors, staff and students. I spent 21 years with you and your martial arts school and it absolutely played a crucial role in who I am today. Dr. Dunphy, you were like a second father to me and I will always be grateful for your wisdom and guidance throughout my life. To all other Shinbukan seniors: Shari Dunphy, Louis Begue, Richard Sacco, Dave Ball, JJ Ramirez, Catherine Nelson, John Green, Amanda Froelich, Christian McAndrew, Tim Ailes, Curtis Duffey, Mike Hall - thank you all for bleeding, sweating, teaching and training with me for many years. Arigato gozaimasu!

A sincere thank-you to the great author of fantasy, J.R.R. Tolkien. It was Tolkien's works, particularly *The Silmarillion*, *The Hobbit* and *The Lord of the Rings* which first inspired me to love writing. Though at the time of reading Tolkien, I never imagined becoming an author, he gave me a love for writing, poetry and storytelling which planted the seeds of authorship within me. Though he is not alive today, my sincerest thank-you goes out to Professor Tolkien as I am not sure I would have ever written anything if he had not written his books.

A very special thanks to the following individuals who helped with elements of creating the book:

- Margaret Lanshe - for sketching the original logo design.
- Rebecca Sinchok - for creating the digital logo of Margaret's sketch and making an awesome image.
- Sofia Vober - for taking my awesome headshot featured on the back cover of this book.
- Angie from Fiverr.com - for designing such an amazing cover! We worked non-stop for 2 days and I couldn't be happier with your work.

A very special thanks to my financial supporters - these individuals contributed monetarily which provided me with the freedom to train, write, and research for this project:

- Lawrence Halmasy, Randall Traub, Dennis, Lisa and Adam McLaughlin, Candace Pryor, Bill & Julie Carrier, David & Kandace Phelps, Howard Clark, Beverly Haws, Charlotte Graf, Virgil Klunder, Sandra Gardner, Curtis Cook, John & Faith Lanshe, Gabrielle Lanshe, Kenneth Choate, Barbara Tysell, Jerry & Leslie Flohr, Rachel Matties, Nick Pappas, Susan Brenner, Steve Bentz, Roland Camacho, Curtis Duffey, Cynthia Julius, Christine Angione, Nato Jacobson, Tonya McCaulley, Lori DeVille, Susan Gardner-Hill, Andrew Halmasy, Brenda Brown, Brittany Buck, Jill Eckroad, Mark Highsmith, Katerina Larson, and Tory Vest.

The following individuals deserve a special thank-you as well:

- Scott and Kimberly Ostrowski - for providing guidance & a listening ear to me as I went through a dark time of loss
- Gina Martinez - for your sacrifice in bringing the truth to light and sharing the truth with me - thank you
- Cynthia Julius – for being a great teacher who first introduced me into the world of higher knowledge and thinking that greatly shaped my identity as a man. Thank you.

The following are individuals who I admire, but did not interview for this project whom I would like to thank for their service and body of work in the protector community:

Bob Duggan, Kelly McCann, Dakota Meyer, Terry Trahan, John Douglas, Steven Pressfield, Lord Moran, Gen. James "Mad Dog" Mattis, Marc MacYoung, Kyle Carpenter, Sheriff David Clarke, Kris Paranto, Larry Vickers, Gabby Franco, Greg Ellifritz, Allen West, Barret Kendrick, Christopher Bronzi, Craig Douglas, David Scott-Donelan, Donovan Campbell, Dr. Bill Lewinski, Gov. Eric Greitins, Guy Gruters, Jason Hanson, Joe Bail, John "Jocko" Willink, Kevin Davis, Kyle Lamb, Mad Max Mullen, John Plaster, Ray Sprankle, Rubon Munoz, R. Lee Ermey, Sandra Froman, Tatiana Whitlock, Tim Dimoff, Tom Satterley, Travis Haley, and Tim Kennedy.

The following individuals are being given special recognition for having inspired me in an extraordinary way now or at one time in my life:

The Blessed Virgin Mary, St. Augustine of Hippo, St. Thomas Aquinas, St. Francis de Sales, C.S. Lewis, John O'Leary, Dave

Ramsey, Les Brown, Tanya Brown, Professor Joe Martin, Sean Astin, Kacy Catanzaro, Jessie Graff, Rudy Ruettiger, Lou Holtz, Robert Cialdini, Dr. Ben Carson, Dr. Gary Chapman, Lindsey Stirling, Fr. L. Campbell, Professor Jordan Peterson, Lila Rose, Jason Vale, Cassie Jaye, Steven Crowder, Simon Sinek, Dale Partridge, Colm Wilkinson, Howard Shore, Hans Zimmer, Peter Jackson, John Williams, Rachel Cruze, Phil Mickelson, Sandra Joseph, the cast, staff and crew of CBS' *Criminal Minds*, The Piano Guys, Linda Eder, John Maxwell, George Lucas, Thomas Sowell, Eurielle, John Lennox, Dr. David Menton, Mel Robbins, Joe Cross, Peter Hollens, Anthony Warlow, Dr. Jason Lisle, and Ennio Morricone.

In no particular order, I would like to acknowledge all of the following individuals for having a positive role in my life. All of whom, in their own way, made a difference in the forging of my character and life story which led to the production and completion of this book:

Aaron Shaffer, Abby Anderson, Abby Wahl, Adriana Young, Alaina Thiel, Alex and Amelia Lerma, Allie Green, Allison Fassinger,

Amanda Drouhard, Amanda Thorne, Amanda Wahl, Amy Jordan, Amy Rice, An Pham, Andrea Young, Andrew Bolzman, Angel Marie Monachelli, Angela Thomas, Annabelle Sew, Annette Marsolais, Anni Keffer, Annie Carney, Antonia Gore, Ashley Gordon, Ashley Soyk, Ashley Yassell, Audra Brace, Audrey Wahl, Autumn Terry, Barbara Tysell, Bart Christian, Ben and Jennifer Linville, Ben Gioia, Bethany Noble, Bill and Betty Flohr, Bill Caldon, Bill Fairman, Bob and Connie Pacanovsky, Boots Dobbins, Branavan and Braveen Ragunanthan, Brett Judd, Brianna Habel, Brock Sandrock, Caeli Ridge, Caleb Kisner, Cameron Traub, Carlie Sue, Cat Crews, Cathy Guinovart, Chad White, Chelsey Kirkland, Chris and Elisabeth Scappatura, Chris Cooper, Chris Warner, Chris Wurst, Christian Johnson, Christina White, Christopher Frazier, Cindy McLane, Claire McBride, Cole Meller, Craig Duswalt, Cristin McKinley, Crystal Parra, Dan and Laureen O'Donnell, Dan and Lois Cricks, Daniel and Ivy Bino, Danielle Boggs, Danny Brassell, Daryl Hershberger, Dave Van Horn, Davy Tyburski, Denny Goodwill, Don Alley, Donna Krech, Doug Marques, Dylan Vanas, Eldonna Lewis Fernandez, Elise Delegrange, Elizabeth Brooke, Elliot Wainess, Emily Cribb, Emily May-Roberts, Emma Court, Eric Shelly, Erika Vosbeck, Erin Gulling, Ethan Wahl, Fallon Brace, Forest and Stormy

Hamilton, Forrest Bryant, Frank Curtin, Gennifer Akroyd, Genny Masti, Glen Stromberg, Greg and Stephanie Dieringer, Greg Flohr, Heather Dennington, Hilda Chavez, Hillary Flohr, Jackie Klayko, James and Tirzah Burns, Jamie Dickenson, Jamie Klunder, Jamilla Brooks, Janie Lidey, Jason Basuil, Jason Shannon, Jeff and Barb Wahl, Jeff Dousharm, Jeff Kline, Jeff Watson, Jennie Dieter, Jennifer Rhodes, Jeremiah and Laura Hruby, Jerry and Leslie Flohr, Jerry Rizzo, Jesica Ahlberg, Jessica Klunder, Jimmal Ball, Jimmy Meeks, John "Peachy" Marshall, John and Jeannie Harasin, John Formica, John Parks, John Paxton, John Powers, John Turnbull, Jona Xiao, Jonathan Sprinkles, Judith Juvancic-Heltzel, Judy Drouhard, Justin Wrubel, Kara Cooper-Garland, Katrina Tripp, Kelby Bosshardt, Kelsie Ahbe, Kendal Hollady, Kennedy McDermott, Kenneth Choate, Kennon Williams, Kristen Laemmer, Kristen Traub, Kristin Olson, Kyle and Madi Gray, Kyle Konet, Kyle Whiddon, Latoya Higgenbottom, Laura Richardson, Lauren Osco, Lauren Walter, LaVonna Roth, Libby Matthews, Lindsey and Rick Cope, Lori Tsey, Lynn Wagers, Maria Maculaits, Marian Blazina, Marissa Dubina, Mark and Grace Demaree, Mark Jackson, Mark Sweeney Jackson, Marti Reed, Marty and Rita Fassinger, Mary Drouhard, Matt and Maria Granados, Meghan Chapin, Melanie Anderson,

Melanie Harvey, Melanie Marie, Melissa Smith, Merv Plank, Michael Delegrange, Michael Erpenbach, Michael Harvey, Michelle Payton Chapman, Mike and Janine Delegrange, Mike and LeAnn Fritz, Mike Davis, Mike Warner, Nathan Klayko, Nicholas and Amanda Bayerle, Nick and Beth Nussen, Nick Granados, Nick Smith, Nicole Dietz-Hunt, Nicole Kline, Nolan Habel, Oksana Borychkevych, Patricia Coe, Paul and Rebekah Watson, Phillip Lance, Quincey Long, Rachel Robinson, Rachele Kappler, Raj Dhamrait, Ralph and Karil Klayko, Rennie Gabriel, Rhonda Kirby, Rich Swad, Richard Barrier, Rob and Kristen Habel, Rob Shallenberger, Robert Brace, Robin Roseberry, Rodger and Deb Emerson, Ron Otterstetter, Ryan Brennan, Sarah Flohr, Scott and Jenny Hammerle, Scott and Susan Brenner, Scott Keffer, Sebastian Flohr, Shaniee Parker, Stacey Buser, Steve Peck, Stuart Maue, Tabitha Miller, Ted Prodomou, Terri Hardin Jackson, Theresa Krafcheck, Thomas Schmidt, Thuli Mphasa, Tim and Teresa Hodgkiss, Toby Jurging, Tom and Deb Sterling, Tom Olson, Tommy and Jackie Brennan, Tony Granados, Traceylee Goane, Travis Brown, TW and Heather Walker, Veronica Judith, Dr. Victor Pinheiro, Vivian Thakhuli, Wayne Sheaffer, Wendy Sweet, Will Harvey, Zarah Al-noubani, Zipporah Evania.

I would like to thank *First Tactical* for making such awesome gear. I have been using a 3-Day backpack, laptop case, and service gloves I purchased from them for years and I love them. The quality is excellent and lots of people have asked me where I got my gear. I do not earn affiliate commissions from them, I refer people to them simply because I have used and continue to use their products to my great satisfaction. You can check them out by visiting their website: https://www.firsttactical.com/

The Ideal Professional Speaker for Your Event

Speaking is my passion and my favorite way to share the principles of *Anatomy of a Warrior* with people just like you. I have the great honor of being able to speak for groups ranging from a handful of attendees for local organizations to thousands of attendees at major, national conferences.

If you believe that it is your duty to protect your people and organization from violence, adversity, and suffering, I would love for you to invite me to visit and speak.

I look forward to speaking for you and your people!

Email: Info@AlexLanshe.com

Website: https://www.AlexLanshe.com/Speaking

Foreword – Lt. Col. Dave Grossman

You hold in your hands one of the most important books of our times. I call these times the "Warrior Renaissance". In my science fiction series, *The Two Space War*, I depict warriors 600 years in the future who refer to this period at the end of the twentieth century and the beginning of the twenty-first century as a "Warrior Renaissance." I sincerely believe that future generations will look back on this period as a renaissance, a period of remarkable progress in which the full potential of the human factors in combat began to be fully realized. It is entirely possible that elite warriors 100 years from now will look back on these years as the era in which we began to discover this untapped human potential.

With this remarkable book, Alex Lanshe has established himself as the chronicler, the scribe, for this Warrior Renaissance. *Anatomy of a Warrior* is based on two and a half years of research, and 120 interviews with some of the greatest minds of this era. Never has the distilled wisdom of so many professional warriors and scholars of human violence from all across the spectrum of service (Police,

Military and Private Sector) been captured for one book. More important than the source of his wisdom is the manner in which Alex has presented it. This book takes a revolutionary approach to preventing human violence by focusing on developing the virtue of the individual warrior. Beginning with the foundational concept that a protector and his tactics are only as good as the virtues that give life to his actions, this book codifies the seven most important virtues that a protector must strive to live by in order to *prevent*, *prepare*, and *protect* from violence. To protect not just individuals, but to protect our very way of life. These virtues hold true for the professional protector as well as the civilian who simply wants to safeguard his or her family.

You will find many books on many topics that seem to operate in a vacuum. But the best books on any subject are those that "stand on the shoulders of giants" and build on that which has already been achieved, skillfully weaving past wisdom together with new information and new insight, to create a book that is greater than the sum of its parts. *That* is what Alex has done in this book; incorporating, applying, and recommending some of the great minds and great works that have been previously written on this vital subject. No other book has ever come even close to doing what this book has achieved - and we have never needed this book more than we do now.

Wherever you are, right now, as you read these words, you can probably look up and see some of the things our society has done to prepare for the threat of fire. Some form of "fire code" has influenced the building you are in, right now. You can probably see smoke alarms, fire sprinklers, and possibly fire-exit signs. A fire extinguisher or a fire hydrant may be directly in sight. By some estimates, half the construction cost of a modern building will go into meeting the requirements of the "fire code". Fireproof or fire-retardant material for the structure of the building, and for internal furnishings, versus the cheapest alternative. Electrical system brought up to fire code. Double the electrical system in some buildings, to run wiring to all fire-exit signs and smoke alarms. Fire sprinkler system under pressure for the lifetime of the building. The "fire alarm" in many buildings is an amazing expense all by itself, with a separate network of wiring, running through our civilization, from every building to the local fire station. From our youngest days we did "fire drills" and perhaps you were taught "stop, drop and roll" in case you ever caught on fire. Vast amounts of money, time and effort go into preparing for fire. In the United States, every year around 300 people are killed by fire, but approximately 17,000 are killed by violence. If we can spend all this money and time to prepare for fire (and we should) how much more so should we prepare for violence? And yet, the comparison between fire and violence completely breaks down, when we consider the psychological effects of "natural factors" versus violence.

During the 9-11 attacks in the United States, terrorists murdered over 3,000 citizens. The stock market crashed, the US invaded two nations, and our world changed dramatically. That same year, over 30,000 Americans were killed in traffic accidents, and it didn't change anything. Because they were *accidents*. The *Diagnostic and Statistical Manual of the American Psychiatric Association* (the "Bible" of psychiatry and psychology) tells us that whenever the "cause" of a traumatic event is "human in nature" the degree of psychological trauma is "usually more severe and long lasting." Ask yourself how you would response to these two scenarios:

- A tornado (or earthquake or fire or tsunami) hits your house while you are gone, and puts your whole family in the hospital. How do you feel about that? Most people would say that they are glad their family had survived.

- A gang hits your house while you are gone, and beats your whole family into the hospital. How do you feel about that one? Most people whole have to admit that there is a vast difference between these two scenarios, and we have to admit to ourselves that preparation for violence.

Consider:

- The attack on the World Trade Center on September 11, 2001, with 2,996 dead. Generally considered the most horrendous terrorist attack in history.

- 69 murdered and 120 wounded on Utoya, Norway, in 2011, in the most horrendous massacre by a single individual with a firearm. (Still significantly more than the 59 murdered in the Las Vegas Mandalay Massacre in 2017.)

- 15 murdered by a student in Winnenden, Germany, 2009, in the worst massacre by a juvenile in history.

This is not some ancient history nor some distant land. This is us. This is now. In the US, the FBI tells us that the number of mass murders are doubling every decade, and the average body count is going up. You do not have to go any further than the front page of your newspaper to find similar examples in your own part of the world. There is a new twist to terrorism: It's called body count. Whether the perpetrators are school killers, workplace killers, or international terrorists, they are not interested in negotiating; their only goal is to kill as many people as humanly possible.

The defining challenge of the years to come is to protect our loved ones, our students, our customers, our employees, our civilization and our very way of life from violence, in the same way that we protect them from fire. But wait. The sky is *not* falling. It is within our ability to meet this challenge. There are warriors and warrior-scholars who will rise to the challenge and guide us on virtuous paths to defend our civilization in these dark hours. In 1945, Lord Moran, in the early days of the Warrior Renaissance, published his seminal book, *Anatomy of Courage.* It is so very appropriate that now, at the peak of this Renaissance, Alex Lanshe has given us his *Anatomy of a Warrior.*

J.R.R. Tolkien was a man very much like Lord Moran. Influenced by the same historical experiences, he gave us the great classic of our times, the great warrior epic, *The Lord of the Rings.* In that book can be found these classic words of hope in the darkest hour:

> *Not all that is gold doth glitter,*
>
> *Not all those who wander are lost.*
>
> *The old that is strong does not whither,*
>
> *And the deep roots are not touched by the frost.*

Now, in this dark hour, let us tap the strength that is drawn from those deep roots that have endured the bitter frost, let us seek out the old that is strong and does not whither- the old ways, the ways of the virtuous warrior -- in order to answer the challenge of the age. And thus, with all my heart, I encourage you to not just read, but study and apply this groundbreaking book, this powerful reexamination of classical warrior virtues that Alex Lanshe has given us, to create virtuous modern day warriors and leaders to serve on the front lines of a civilization combating violence and evil.

Dave Grossman

Lt. Col., U.S. Army (ret.)

Author of *On Killing, On Combat,* and *Assassination Generation*

Director, Killology Research Group, www.killology.com

Bio

Lt. Col. Dave Grossman is a former West Point psychology professor, Professor of Military Science, and an Army Ranger who is the author of *On Killing, On Combat,* and *Assassination Generation.* Col. Grossman's work has been translated into many languages, and his books are required or recommended reading in colleges, military academies, and police academies around the world, to include the US Marine Corps Commandant's reading list and the FBI Academy reading list. His research was cited by the President of the United States in a national address after the Littleton, Colorado school massacre, and he has testified before the US Senate, the US Congress, and numerous state legislatures. He has served as an expert witness and consultant in state and Federal courts, to include UNITED STATES vs. TIMOTHY MCVEIGH.

He helped train mental health professionals after the Jonesboro school massacre, and he was also involved in counseling or court cases in the aftermath of the Paducah, Springfield, and Littleton school shootings. He has been called upon to write the entry on "Aggression and Violence" in the *Oxford Companion to American Military History,* three entries in the *Academic Press Encyclopedia of Violence, Peace and Conflict* and has presented papers before the national conventions of the American Medical Association, the American Psychiatric Association, the American Psychological Association, and the American Academy of Pediatrics.

He also has published several novels, and he has five US patents to his name. He has a black belt in Hojutsu, the martial art of the firearm, and has been inducted into the USA Martial Arts Hall of Fame.

Today he is the director of the Killology Research Group (www.killology.com), and in the wake of the 9/11 terrorist attacks he has been on the road 250 days a year, for 20 years since his retirement from the US Army, training elite military and law enforcement organizations worldwide about the reality of combat, and he has written extensively on the terrorist threat with articles published in the Harvard Journal of Law and Public Policy and many leading law enforcement journals.

Introduction

This book is based on 2.5 years of dedicated research. I conducted phone or video interviews with 120 current or former professional protectors who serve or have served in various roles such as:

- US Air Force
- US Navy
- US Army
- US Marines
- US Coast Guard
- US Army Rangers
- US Navy SEALS
- US Green Berets
- US Marshals
- US Presidential Advisors
- Sheriffs and Sheriff's Deputies
- Police Officers, Highway Patrol Officers & Police Trainers
- Chiefs of Police
- SWAT (including officers who responded at the Columbine and Virginia Tech Massacres)
- Texas Rangers

- Executive Protectors

- Firefighters & Paramedics

- PhD Psychologists

- Real World Violence Survivors (Professional and Civilian)

- International Special Forces Trainers

- Founders of Protective Groups and Organizations

- Agents or Trainers of Government Agents such as the NSA, CIA and FBI

- Prisoners of War

- Nationally Recognized Speakers & Authors

- Leading Authorities on Violence and Survival Strategies

- Expert Witnesses

- Firearms Trainers

- Homicide Detectives

- Survivors of Foreign Civil Wars

- Medal of Valor Recipients (Police) and recipients of numerous Military Medals such as the Purple Heart and Bronze Star

- Martial Arts Practitioners of various disciplines

- Competitive Shooting Champions (including World Champions)

The interviews ranged in time from 13 minutes to 60+ minutes. Each person was asked the same question regarding what characteristics and virtues are most essential to succeeding as a protector (in addition to various follow up questions - some of which were predetermined and others which arose spontaneously during the conversation). The chapters are organized from the most referenced virtue (chapter 1) to the least referenced virtue (chapter 7).

The following information is written in my own words and is not a transcript of each interview. As such, not every interviewee will be directly quoted or referenced within the text. A full list with the names, backgrounds and contact information for the interviewees can be found in the back of the book.

It is important to note that each person was interviewed as an individual and they were not speaking in any official capacity for their respective organizations or groups unless they were authorized to do so. All direct quotes of the interviewees are their opinions and do not necessarily reflect the beliefs of the author or of any of the organizations or groups they belong to now, at any time in the past, or at any time in the future. This book contains the collective wisdom and experience of 120 of the world's finest protectors and warriors. You honor me and them by reading this book and seeking to acquire their hard fought wisdom for your own life. I applaud you. You now possess the virtue blueprint necessary to be a good protector. Whether you have been a protector in the professional realm for decades or are a young civilian wondering if you have the right stuff, this book seeks to help you become a new protector or to become an even better protector and warrior than you already are.

Whether you seek to protect your family, business, school, place of employment, country, yourself or innocent lives, the *Anatomy of a Warrior* virtues can help you do so. The world needs virtuous warriors more than ever before - thank you for embarking on this journey with me.

Live with Virtue!

Chapter 0: I Believe . . .

I believe that living virtuously can protect human lives and prevent death and suffering. I believe it is my duty, your duty, and each person's duty to become the best warrior and protector you can be to make your area of the world a little bit safer. This subject is important to me because I have studied martial arts and the science of violence for more than 20 years and have been teaching and instructing for over a decade. I cannot remember life without martial training. I've done all manner of training, from National Rifle Association (NRA) pistol certifications to classical Japanese swordsmanship; from fighting in karate sparring tournaments to getting shot with airsoft pistols in live, role-playing, force-on-force training.

More than Physical Training

While the physical training is quite important and should not be neglected, the subject of this book highlights another element of protecting people from violence that you should be focus on: the seven virtues of the warrior heart. I realized one day that all the physical training in the world does you little good if you lack the proper virtues that inform and compose your character. Why?

Because your character and the virtues thereof inform your behavior and your actions. It stands to reason, then, that if you want to become an even better protector than you already are, you should strive to acquire these virtues.

The Question

What virtues are the most essential for a warrior to live by in order to prepare for, protect against and prevent human violence? That is the question that this book seeks to answer. It does this by focusing on developing the virtue of the individual protector.

Research

To answer that question I did 2½ years of research by interviewing 120 top professional protectors from military, police, and private sectors (check out the amazing interviewee list at the back of the book) and asked them that very question. I boiled down what all 120 protectors said and found seven common virtues. I codified them and put them into this book, which I now use as the platform from which I seek to fulfill my life's mission of preventing unnecessary death and suffering. In other words, neutralizing interpersonal violence and chaos.

Disclaimer

It should be noted that these interviewees were not claiming they live by these virtues perfectly—they don't and neither do I. These virtues are the ideals, the standards that we should strive to reach as closely as possible. They are the target we are aiming and firing at. The targets serve as the objective standards that give shooting meaning, context, and reference. If you just started shooting but had no goal, no direction, and no targets, how could you measure how well you were doing? How could you tell if you hit the bull's-eye? Just like in shooting, some days you nail the bull's-eye and you seemingly can't miss, but other days, you miss your target area or the entire target. This does not stop you from returning to the range next week, however. Virtue is like this—you will have some days when you hit every target and other days when you don't fare so well. Dust yourself off and keep going.

Why You Should Care

Why should you care about virtue? Why is using virtue as a neutralizing tool against violence so important? Can't you just go get a concealed carry permit and then voilà, you are safe? If only that was how it worked. I believe that violence is a much more broad-spectrum issue than just learning how to deal with a home invasion or going to the range and shooting your pistol. Violence and conflict happen all the time and take numerous forms, from road rage to home invasions, and from policing a beat to fighting wars overseas. Whether you are a professional soldier or a stay-at-home mother, virtue is necessary to handle and deal with these conflicts and chaos.

Why Should You Care?

You should care about studying and honing these virtues because they do not just prepare you to face interpersonal violence, but can be used to great effect to battle the daily challenges you experience. A home invasion is, statistically speaking, a rare occurrence, but putting the children to bed, doing your taxes, going to work each day, fighting traffic jams, making sure you budget your finances correctly, and so on are tasks you perform with regularity. The warrior virtues give meaning, purpose, and vitality to those tasks as well. You should care about pursuing these warrior virtues because they will give meaning and purpose to your everyday struggles and challenges. You should care because while you simultaneously grow in virtue, you become more able to protect and keep your loved ones safe from threats of all natures: physical, emotional, mental, and spiritual.

Perhaps most importantly, a lack of virtue can directly or indirectly lead to violence, whereas the application of these virtues could have easily prevented it from escalating to that point. I would rather prevent violence before it happens than deal with it once it has started. Don't you agree? Focusing on the virtues outlined in this book will have a tremendous preventative effect, much like taking your vitamins to prevent disease.

Legal Obligation

I make absolutely zero guarantees that living by or not living by these virtues will or will not prevent or help you to combat violence. As with anything, you must actually do the work, and I cannot make you do it. Even then, you could do everything right before, during, and after a violent encounter and still end up dying. That is life. Bad things happen to good people, and sometimes there is nothing you could have done to stop it or alter the outcome. This does not mean the pursuit of virtue and martial training is meaningless, however— quite the contrary. You can drastically mitigate your risk and vulnerability by seeking out quality martial training and by living according to these virtues, but I cannot make any guarantees. Your life is in your hands, not mine, or those of any other author, speaker, or interviewee for this book. We cannot control you, nor can we assure you of safety. Do the work, be vigilant, and say your prayers.

Who Can Pursue These Virtues?

The good thing about virtue is that anyone can be virtuous. Yes, that means you too. Many people lack the physical skills to be competent and skilled soldiers or fighters, but physical injuries, birth defects, or other physical limitations do not stop you from being a protector and a warrior if you focus on forging virtue. I believe that intentionally living according to these seven virtues can neutralize and prevent death, suffering, and help you to overcome adversity and chaos. This discovery makes you a vital piece in the bigger picture of keeping people safe. Whether or not you live with virtue truly does matter and has an effect on the greater society and world at large. You and your actions are not insignificant.

What is Virtue?

You may be asking, "What is virtue?" Good question! Some synonyms are morality, righteousness, and goodness. Google defines virtue as "behavior showing high moral standards." I find these synonyms and definition unsatisfying. Virtue means so much more than that. I define virtue as:

> Virtue is a way of being; the perfect combination and
>
> harmony of action, wisdom, intention, reason, and will

working towards bringing about the greatest good in accord with ultimate truth. Virtue is lived. Virtue is the noblest expression and manifestation of human nature.

I Believe

I believe that virtue is the unseen and unspoken foundation for all of civilization. If it erodes too far, society cannot function and all order breaks down. Virtue ensures order, and order prevents chaos. Violence lives in chaos. It stands to reason then that if you live with more virtue and decrease the amount of chaos in your own life, violence and/or its likelihood, will decrease. It likewise stands to reason that if millions of people make this same virtuous change in their lives, all of society would experience a decrease in violence collectively. Do I believe we can ever get rid of all interpersonal violence? No. But I believe we can reduce the number of victims. The first step toward living a virtuous life is knowing what virtue is and which virtues to intentionally strive for. No matter how badly you think you may struggle with being virtuous, you are capable of being virtuous but you must believe that you are in control of yourself. You must believe the buck ultimately stops with you. If you believe this, then you have the power to shape your future and to intentionally focus on practicing virtue.

Virtue Referrals

Think of forging your virtue like a referral system in business. If you get one client to refer just one more client, you now have two clients. If that new client gives you just two referrals, you now have four clients. Your client pool has doubled! What would that do for your business? Good things, right? So now imagine your virtuous acts being like referrals. If you live with virtue and inspire just one person to live with virtue too, we now have two virtuous people. If that new person inspires just two people, now we have four people living virtuously who were not previously doing so. Continue to run the math out, and you can see that this could have far-reaching consequences and gives each person, including you, a vital role to play. Your actions matter, whether or not you live with virtue matters! As I wrote earlier, virtue is the very thing that allows human beings to live in peace and harmony. Virtue is what allows for heroic acts of grandeur, like rescuing someone from drowning (look at the amazing acts of heroism in the aftermath of Hurricane Harvey in Houston, Texas, for example) and the simple, quiet acts of heroism like lovingly rocking your baby to sleep even though you have been awake for 24 hours. I believe that this message of virtue is foundational to a healthy society. I believe it is my calling to propagate this message and help you to become a virtuous protector and warrior.

The Void of Virtue

I believe that there is a lack of virtue in our nation. For example: Employers are always complaining that they can't seem to find enough what? Good people to hire. Employees are always complaining that they can't find any what? Good bosses or leaders to follow. I have heard many friends complaining about the dating scene, insomuch as they can't find enough what? Good people to date. What do they all mean? "Good" employees, and "good" leaders and "good" dates? What do they mean? They mean virtue. When you say: "I can't find enough good __" what you really mean is: "I can't find enough *virtuous* employees, leaders, spouses, politicians, artists, role models," and so on. The void of virtue is everywhere, but the good news is that where there are voids, there exist opportunities to fill those voids. We live in a time of unprecedented opportunity.

What Are You?

Aristotle once said, "We are what we repeatedly do." I firmly believe this. If you consistently practice virtue, you become virtuous. If you consistently practice vice, you become viceful (a new word I just invented). Gandhi once said, "Be the change you want to see in the world." And I agree that if we want a "better" world, each of us must commit to practicing virtue in our own lives.

Who is *Anatomy of a Warrior* for?

With these things in mind, who can benefit from this book? Anyone who wants to finally take responsibility for their life and start *being* someone virtuous. There are some specific categories of people that may benefit the most from this book however. Which of these categories do you belong to?

1. Military, police, executive protectors, government agents, and others: This is written primarily for you. Your profession already demands that you protect others, and if you actually live and embody these virtues, you will be able to do a better job doing what you have chosen as your profession. I firmly believe that if you dutifully live out these virtues you will prevent more death and suffering, do your job with more joy, increase the likelihood of having a longer career, and develop the character that can withstand any evil that visits you. The virtues outlined in this book, if practiced, will help you to protect yourself, your family, your teammates, your country, and our world.

1. First responders, paramedics, firefighters, nurses, Hippocratic Oath swearers, midwives, healers, and medicinalists (another word I just invented) will benefit highly from this book too. You seek to cure ills and stop suffering, and if you embody these virtues, I believe you will be able to do your job and live your life's calling more effectively.

1. Mothers, what greater task could there be than to raise and protect your children? You will benefit highly from living by these virtues as you guide and lead your children through the struggles of life. Your children will greatly benefit from your virtue as well.

1. Fathers, what greater task than to be the bedrock of protection and sustenance for your wives and children? You will benefit greatly from embodying these virtues so that you can lead by example and be a truly virtuous role model for your wives and children.

1. Second Amendment supporters, you will benefit greatly from pairing your zeal for firearms and guns with the virtues that allow you to know when to act and how to guard against impetuousness. Your gun won't do you any good if you use it incorrectly or at the wrong time. You may already have the

physical skills needed to protect, so now, if you pair those up with solid virtue to inform right actions, you will become an even better warrior.

1. Teachers, educators, daycare specialists, professors, and mind-shapers, you have been tasked with protecting and safeguarding the future - our children. That may require you to stop a violent attacker but it likely will not. What our children desperately need are virtuous leaders, mentors and role models to guide them in right conduct so that they can become virtuous citizens and human beings. Your task is no small one and your responsibility is great. These virtues will serve you well on your life mission to educate the youth.

1. Pro-lifers, who could be in greater need of protection than the unborn? You do a great service each day you strive to keep an unborn baby safe and you will find the virtues contained in this book quite helpful for you to contemplate and live out in your life. These virtues will help you to carry on in your journey and the unborn will benefit from your effort.

Who is a Protector?

If you feel that you do not fit into any of the categories I have listed so far, I want to tell you something one of the interviewees told me. I interviewed a man named Rob Erikson. He is a former United States Marine. He told me during our interview that: "Everyone is a protector to a certain extent." I firmly believe this. I believe that you have the capacity to be a protector of yourself and others. You may lack the physical skills, but as this book will show, protecting human lives does not always look like Superman punching the bad guy and flying away in triumph. Even someone who is a quadriplegic can protect others if he is virtuous. You may have never felt any calling to be "protector" at all—but you are one. You don't need a special calling to be one—anyone can take up the task. In fact, I believe it is your duty to do so. If you need to be given permission, *boom*! I give you permission to be a protector.

Definition of Protector

By "protector," I mean and define it as anyone who willingly takes up the personal task of seeking and doing what is necessary to protect someone or a group of persons from violence, death, and suffering. Someone who takes a sick friend to the hospital to get medicine is being a protector. A mother who ensures her children are properly fed and nourished is being a protector. A father who works 70+ hours a week to ensure that his family has enough money for their survival is a being a protector. The police officer responding to an active mass murderer at a school is being a protector. A soldier overseas protecting our nation is being a protector. Notice I've said, "is being" and not simply "is." That's because being a protector requires just that, being. You must *do* it. You have to LIVE/ACT/DO something to be a protector. It is not a title you simply claim or a moniker that is awarded to you—you must do the work, perform the actions, and exhibit the behavior of being a protector. A protector is something you must be—it is not a badge that, once placed on you, magically sticks to you forever. Being a protector is a lot like being a shark; you need to keep doing it in order to be one. A shark that stops swimming will drown, quickly decompose, or be eaten by scavengers and cease to be a shark.

The Never-ending War

Being a protector, like the pursuit of virtue, is a never-ending war or pursuit, and being a protector is a lifelong choice. Lt. Col. Dave Grossman perhaps said it best:

> **"Sometimes the ultimate love is not to sacrifice your life, but to live a life of sacrifice."**

The small, repeated choice of doing the right thing to ensure the survival and well-being of others is what makes you a protector—to live that life of sacrifice. You might be thinking, "A life of sacrifice? I don't know, Alex; that seems pretty hard. How will I always have the strength to go on?" That is the truly great thing about virtue; it is a bottomless well. You can never reach in, drink too deeply, and dry up the well. No matter how much virtue you take from it, an infinite supply sits beneath it, waiting for you and others to claim it. The more virtuous you are, the more virtuous you can become in the future. It is truly limitless. If you had an infinite source of energy and ammunition, you wouldn't fear going into battle. While our physical tools may expire, break down, or flee us, your virtue cannot leave you unless you consent to its going.

What Do You Really Want?

Isn't this what you've been craving all your life? Something that is endless, boundless, and infinite? I don't know about you, but all my worldly pursuits like acquiring more money, eating nice food, stocking up on possessions, going on vacations, and so on never seem to satisfy in and of themselves. Those things, of their own accord, are not evil but if they are pursued as ends in themselves, they cannot make you content, happy, or fulfilled. You will always want more and will never be satisfied. Virtue, on the other hand, when practiced, makes you thirst for more and yet it is a thirst that while unquenchable in the ultimate sense, always fills you up and makes you satisfied when you take a new draught of it. Consuming more virtue, if you will, does leave you wanting more but in a fulfilling and satiating way. Virtue begets virtue just as vice begets vice.

My Gift to You

This book is my gift to you, and I pray you take its principles to heart and apply them. Our sad, broken world desperately needs to be reminded of the power of living a virtuous life. My central premise and contention is that striving after these seven virtues will prevent unnecessary human death and suffering, allow us to embrace and benefit from the suffering that cannot be avoided, and if you should ever have to engage in real violence, and you survive, these virtues will give you a greater ability to survive the emotional, mental, and spiritual aftermath. I am on a mission to share these virtues as much as I can with anyone who believes what I believe.

My Vision

My vision is that everyone learns to live intentionally by these virtues and to put them into practice in their daily lives as much as possible.

More specifically, I want to get this book in front of 25,000 people a year from the date of release. I will help to bring about this vision by writing books, doing interviews on media outlets such as radio, television, podcasts, and so on, and by delivering talks, speeches, and presentations to like-minded groups who believe what I believe. Whether the group is for youth in high school or universities or big businesses and corporations, whether I am speaking to only one person in a private consultation, a few dozen in a small group at a local club, or thousands in a huge keynote presentation, I share the warrior virtues of this book and am committed to reaching as many people as I can through these media.

Will You Take Up My Cause with Me?

I want professional protectors to take up this task with me—soldiers, military, cops, and executive protectors. I want doctors, nurses, firefighters, paramedics, healers, and midwives to take up this task with me. I want politicians, journalists, artists, celebrities, professors, lawyers, judges, and public servants to take up this task with me. I want mothers, fathers, grandparents, children, siblings, and coworkers to take up this task with me. Do you believe what I believe? Do you believe that protecting what you love is your responsibility? Do you believe that warrior virtue can neutralize unnecessary death, suffering and violence? I do. Where do I come off taking on such a task? I do not know. I am just a man. One man. But if we all thought that way, the world would have given in to despair long ago. I refuse to do that. I refuse to capitulate to evil and the forces of darkness. I refuse to allow the bad guys to win. I'll be damned before I sit back and do nothing. Even if all I can do is to keep my own heart pure, by God I'm going to strive to do that. Am I scared? Of course. The external enemies are many, and facing your own vice and wretchedness isn't a trip to the beach either. But it is my job to face the evil I can face. I'm scared, but being scared doesn't excuse inaction. I have a job to do. You have a job to do. No matter what job that is, if you live according to these warrior virtues, you'll do your job better and ensure more joy and happiness for yourself and others while mitigating violence, death, and suffering.

The Best Way You Can Join Me in My Mission—Real Actions You Can Take Today!

Here are some actions you can take today to help me spread the warrior virtue message:

- Share this book with your family and friends. Share your copy with them or buy them their own as a gift for a birthday, Christmas, or other holiday.

- Give them access to your Kindle or other e-reader.

- Call your local library and ask them to carry a few copies so that your community can read it for free.

- Send me an email requesting to book me for a speaking engagement for your local chamber of commerce, small business, or organization.

- Buy a copy for your work or business and leave it there as a community resource.

- Get a few copies for your doctor's office, dental office, or mechanic's shop waiting room. Your clients will be grateful for something good to read as they wait, and it just might save or change their life.

  - If you do not run the abovementioned offices, please buy a copy and donate it to those offices.

- Buy a copy or two for your local gun range and donate them to the range to keep on hand as a resource for their members.

- Make a list of organizations you have a connection to or know someone of influence in and share the book with them, asking them to promote it to their organization if they like it.

- Buy a few copies and donate them to your local Department of Veterans Affairs facility.

- Follow Anatomy of a Warrior on Facebook and invite your friends to like the page:

  https://www.facebook.com/anatomyofawarrior/

I cannot reach everyone who needs and wants this by myself. **I need your help**. 25,000 people is a lot of people to reach in one year, but with your help, I'm confident we can do it! Thank you for your help and for embarking on the warrior's journey with me.

Live with virtue, my fellow warrior,

Alexander Lanshe

Owner and CEO of Alexander Lanshe LLC

www.AlexLanshe.com

www.AnatomyOfaWarrior.com

info@AlexLanshe.com

P.S. If you have any questions on how to accomplish any of the above listed items, email your question to

info@AlexLanshe.com

Chapter 1: On Fortitude

"Often the test of courage is not to die but live." —

Vittorio Alfieri[1]

Fortitude was the number one virtue most referenced by the 120 interviewees (who shall henceforth be referred to as the 120W). Some people save the best for last, but we shall begin with the best. What is fortitude? Simply stated, fortitude is courage. I am choosing the word *fortitude* because it encompasses several different dimensions to the virtue of courage that I do not believe the word "courage" connotes anymore in the English-speaking world. Fortitude is an older word which has been subject to fewer changes and modern connotations. Google defines fortitude as "courage in pain or adversity." Not a bad definition, but we shall expand on it. As you will see, fortitude has several different ways of being enacted, understood, and viewed. We will be taking a broad spectrum, 360-degree view of fortitude in this chapter.

---

[1] The Forbes Book of Business Quotations, Edited by Edward C. Goodman, (FBB), pg. 175

What is Fortitude?

Consider the first quote. Fortitude is what it takes to get up each morning and keep living. It is what enables you to do your duty well. Many of the 120W talked about duty and how important it is to being a successful protector. The cold hard truth is that the job simply needs to be done. Someone has to do it. If you have the attitude of a warrior, you figure it might as well be you. You clearly possess some measure of fortitude or you would not be reading this book. You courageously got this book hoping it would help you in your personal life – I commend you for acting on this decision. Another angle to examine this first quote from is that sometimes, it is easier to die than it is to keep on living. A warrior pushes through all struggles if he has fortitude. Fortitude communicates a sense of endurance, a sense of perseverance. Fortitude is what allows you to get up each day and do your job well.

The Michael Fletcher Story

Fortitude also contains the great heroic deeds of legend. One of the 120W, Michael Fletcher, exhibited such heroism and courage in his life.

"In 1994, while he was serving as a paratrooper in the U.S. Army's 82nd Airborne Division, an F-16 fighter jet crashed into a plane on the ground, killing 24 soldiers and injuring

130 more. Fletcher sustained third-degree burns to much of his body when the jet fuel he didn't know he had been coated with ignited as he ran toward the crash to help those involved."[2]

Michael was on fire, and yet he was running to help his fellow soldiers! Would you say he exhibited great courage? I would say so. This is fortitude powerfully concentrated into one event. Fortitude shown in such a short or acute time span is often called bravery, courage, mettle, grit or valor. Let us examine Michael's event. What did he do that makes us admire his courage or fortitude? He took action to save his friends. At the heart of fortitude, then, is the ability to take action. Do you think Michael took action that day because it was the right thing to do or because Michael is a "take action" kind of guy? While I believe Michael thought it was the right thing to do, I know from experience and from talking to the 120W that you don't think about such things in the moment. Michael took action because he had been living with fortitude his whole life—he is a man who takes action.

---

[2] https://www.wcs.edu/infocus/2016/10/26/wcs-staff-member-named-hometown-hero/

Can You Do That?

I know what you are thinking: "Gosh, that sure is amazing, Alex! But I've never done anything like that and I don't expect I ever will. How can I ever acquire the virtue of fortitude?" Good question. Let me answer it by asking you a question: Are such acts of valor and bravery required for you to be fortitudinous? No. Remember, we said that fortitude is also the simple act of doing your daily tasks well—of doing your duty. It matters not what this duty is. Faithfully executing it is all that is required for being fortitudinous. The more consistently and diligently you complete your duties, the more courageous you will become, especially if you do your duty with a joyful and humble heart (more on humility in chapter 4) and especially if you continue to do that duty despite obstacles and adversity seeking to stop you. I cannot stress enough that acts of valor and heroism are not forged in one day, and they don't proceed from a vacuum. They come from the repeated, consistent, dutiful execution of actions. At the core of fortitude, then, is the notion of: "The job needs done and I'm the right person for it."

Resist Temptation

Resistance against temptation builds fortitude. Temptation to do the wrong thing; to cheat, lie, steal, or do something immoral rears its ugly head against all of us—you and I are no exceptions. The more you successfully face such temptation and resist it, the more fortitude you acquire. Unfortunately, there is no cheat code for this. You must put in the work and actually face your demons. Truly, this is indeed fortunate, for how would your character grow otherwise? If I could give you "fortitude in a pill," and all you had to do was swallow it down with a cool glass of water, you would not learn the important lessons adversity had to teach you, nor would you gain the necessary experience of fighting your adversity, which would deprive you of wisdom.

Fortitude Applied to the Body

Lt. Col. Dave Grossman told me something interesting in our interview. He talked about hitting the snooze button in the morning (something I know you've never done). He said, "When you hit that snooze button, what are you training your body to do? You're training yourself to quit when you don't feel like going on." I submit to you that one way you can become more fortitudinous is by gaining control of your physical body. If you set your alarm, get out of bed immediately when it goes off. If you made a checklist of things you absolutely have to get done today, try your best to do them. If you will discipline your body in the small things, you will prepare yourself for extraordinary acts of valor, like those that Michael Fletcher demonstrated. Subduing the body is an oft overlooked point that I implore you not to underestimate. The mind can be very willing but if the body is weak, it may cause you to give up before you should. A good way to look at this would be to imagine that you are the mind of your car and the car is your body. You (the mind) can be as willing as is humanly possible to drive from Boston to Los Angeles, but if the car (the body) is not given the proper fuel, not properly maintained, and has countless broken or failing parts, you will not get very far. Take care of your body and subdue it so that it is not the weak link in your ability to protect.

Fortitude as a State of Being

As you read in Chapter 0, it is important to remember that all virtue is a state of being—they are verbs and actions. You will not become fortitudinous unless you actually *are* fortitudinous. It is something you do, day in and day out. Col. Grossman said:

"A protector is someone who has the courage to do the job day in and day out, year after year, decade after decade."

This is truly the hallmark of a warrior. If this sounds intimidating, that's okay; that simply means you're a normal human being. The secret is that it is still intimidating to people like Col. Grossman, too. (I'm speaking for him here but I think he would agree with me.) It's intimidating in the sense that each day is a new battle. Victory yesterday does not assure victory tomorrow. It is a constant battle, one that can be intimidating to think about. I know it is intimidating for me sometimes. It is tough to keep doing your duty day in and day out, but there is also great pride and satisfaction to be found in a job well done. I feel better when I execute my daily duties than on days when I shirk them. Is this so with you? Also, despite it being intimidating at times, what is the alternative? To quit? To stop being virtuous and exchange virtue for vice? This is detrimental to you and to those you seek to protect. I believe that fortitude is to carry on despite the intimidating nature of the fact that you must do battle each and every day. Fortitude is what pushes you past the weariness.

Fortitude and Fear

Another aspect of fortitude is the ability and willingness to act in spite of fear and uncertainty. It is easier to take action when you know your outcome is assured. It is a different thing entirely when the outcome is unknown. Michael Fletcher did not know if he would live or die, but he acted anyway. To act in the face of fear is the mark of courage.

"Courage is fear holding on a minute longer." —Gen. George Patton[3]

This quote by Patton perfectly sums up what I am describing (leave it to Patton). We all have fear. I want you right now to close your eyes, and picture something you are afraid of. Seriously, close your eyes now and picture it. Get the image as crystal clear in your mind as you can. Feel the fear, and begin to ponder why this particular thing frightens you. Now, let the fear go and come back with me to this page. You just gained more courage than you previously had by actively picturing your fear. Mankind has found no better way to conquer a fear than to face it head on. Pretending it doesn't exist breeds anxiety and worry. Sometimes you can slowly inoculate yourself against your fears. For example, if you are fearful of public speaking, you could start by speaking to a group of four or five friends in your living room instead of in front of 1,000 people as a keynote presenter. However, sometimes your greatest fear will be thrust upon you. If you have avoided facing it up until then, you could become paralyzed with fright, and this is what you as a

---

[3] https://www.brainyquote.com/quotes/authors/g/george_s_patton.html

protector must seek to avoid at all costs. Your life and the lives of the people you love could be at stake. It is ok to have fears. It is not ok to allow those fears to stop you from doing your duty. Your fears do exist, but to act in spite of them is the nature of fortitude. Anyone who tells you they have no fears hasn't done enough examination of conscience. Everyone fears something—loss of respect, loss of celebrity, loss of your vast wealth, being unloved by your children, death, outliving your spouse, etc. Not all fears are physical threats, and as a protector you will face the entire gamut of fears: physical, emotional, social, psychological, and spiritual. It is precisely the fact that you have fear which makes your quest for fortitude noble. We stand in awe of what Michael did that day because he had the choice not to do it. He could have fled, and no one would have blamed him for that. But his courage and fortitude were so great that he put others first. Does this stir your soul and make you wish to strive for such courage? I know it stirs mine.

A Personal Story of Fortitude

I want to tell you a personal story about fortitude, not in comparison to Michael's story, but to demonstrate how fortitude is an important virtue in all of our lives. It happened in 2017 as I completed the research for this book. A man whom I respected, who had served as a mentor and martial arts teacher for 12 years of my life, was exposed to be a fraud, liar, and sexual deviant. This man was running a cult of personality, and I had been one of its most loyal members. I wrote a four-part blog series[4] detailing my experience— how I found out, what was going on in the cult, and a petition to other cult members to leave with me. Imagine what it is like to be told that your father is not your father. Turns out you were adopted, and your parents never told you. How would you feel? I imagine you would feel similar to the way I felt. A person I had trusted, respected highly, gave thousands of dollars to, and spent hundreds of hours training with, was exposed as a fraud. I made countless other sacrifices for this person, only to find out he cared more about my money than my well-being. I was used and played like an instrument, and what a "happy" dance I did. To make matters worse, when I tried to tell others about the reality of the situation, I was met with indifference from most of the cult members. A minority responded to my blogs and at least heard me out. Other members whom I had known for a very long time did not back me up. What made the whole thing even odder is that no one made any attempt to answer the questions I raised in the blogs. Nobody tried to defend

---

[4] https://www.alexlanshe.com/blog/my-personal-story-of-escaping-a-cult-part-1-the-inner-workings

the cult leader from the horrible behavior of which he was accused. No one would debate, and few wanted the truth. I severed all ties and communication with the man and the group I had been a part of for 12 years. I didn't think about it at the time, but I was told by many people who had left the cult years before me (and with whom I reconnected now that I was out) that it took great courage to leave something familiar for the right reasons. I tell my story not to brag to you but to impress upon you that I understand what it takes to do the right thing under pressure when there are consequences on the line. Leaving that cult cost me relationships that I had built over 20, 15, and 10 year spans. When everyone wanted me to do one thing, I had to find the courage to do what was right. It isn't easy to stand up to your friends and tell them the harsh truth they don't want to hear.

How Does My Story Apply to You?

My story applies to you, because you may very well face a similar situation where you are asked—or it is assumed—that you will go along with corruption. I pray that if that time comes, the fortitude you have forged prior to then will be summoned in its full strength to courageously defend the truth, and have no part in corruption. Compromising your character is not worth it.

The Story of Vietnam POW Capt. Charlie Plumb

The next story of fortitude highlights another aspect to fortitude that few consider. It comes from interviewee Capt. Charlie Plumb. Capt. Plumb was a POW in Vietnam for six years. The mission he was flying when he was shot down was to be his last. If he hadn't been shot down, he would have been going home. It was his 75th combat mission, and he was taken prisoner. First, to survive in a POW camp for six years takes incredible fortitude. (Read his book *I'm No Hero*[5] for a full recollection of his experiences as a POW.) This perfectly illustrates the principle of endurance. However, this, in my opinion, is not the most impressive display of fortitude. In my conversation with Capt. Plumb, he mentioned something no one else mentioned. It was something so powerful that I cannot recount it aloud without getting goosebumps. He said that forgiveness was one of the most important virtues for a warrior to possess. (Strictly speaking, forgiveness is not a virtue per se, but it is partly a manifestation of the virtue of fortitude.) Forgiveness? My curiosity piqued, I asked Capt. Plumb to follow up on that point. He proceeded to tell me that while he was a prisoner, he had a subtle

---

[5] https://www.amazon.com/Im-No-Hero-POW-Story/dp/1881886026/ref=sr_1_2?ie=UTF8&qid=1505243620&sr=8-2&keywords=I%27m+No+Hero

and gradual epiphany that in order for him to survive the internment, he needed to forgive his captors and torturers. He said that if he did not forgive them, he knew the anger and bitterness he felt would destroy him. He knew that those feelings could do so much damage to him that even if he physically was liberated from the camp, he would have died emotionally and spiritually long before that. What presence of mind and what grace from God to make this discovery while a prisoner! He told me that forgiveness allows you to see reality for what it truly is. What a powerful statement. As a warrior, your duty is to face reality. Only by facing reality and admitting what it is can you effectively protect yourself and others.

Why Forgiveness?

Why are we talking about forgiveness in the chapter, "On Fortitude?" Because I want you to imagine the internal courage it took for Capt. Plumb to forgive his tormentors. Do it right now. Imagine being in a prison camp, seeing your friends die, feeling the excruciating pain of electrocution and beatings and yet, truly, in the deepest chambers of your heart, you have forgiven the men inflicting that pain and anguish on you and your friends. It boggles my mind. To think of it gives me chills and brings tears to my eyes. I do not know if I could forgive anyone if they were torturing me or one of my six siblings or my parents. Could you? Dear God, what courage this must require! Capt. Plumb demonstrated internal courage. I believe that too often we all think courage is in shooting an enemy on the battlefield. This can be very courageous indeed, but sometimes forgiving that enemy takes even greater courage. This is internal courage and fortitude of the highest caliber, and I pray and hope that I can possess this inner strength. Do you see how fortitude takes on many shapes and forms? It is not simply the solo deeds of heroism, such as shooting down an enemy fighter pilot. It is not just doing your daily duty with diligence. Courage and fortitude extend even into the internal, personal realm, into forgiving your enemies, into forgiving yourself, and into several more realms we will continue to explore.

Courage as the Highest Virtue

"Courage is not simply one of the virtues but the form of every virtue at the testing point." —C.S. Lewis[6]

This quote by C.S. Lewis is perhaps why fortitude is the most important virtue, for it requires fortitude in order to enact any of the other virtues under pressure. You could say that fortitude is the expression and the carrying out of all the other virtues. It is all the

---

[6] FBB, pg. 175

other virtues put into action. It takes courage to love, to be humble, to be just, to be prudent, to have faith, and to be temperate (the other six core virtues of a protector). Stated another way:

"Courage is the supreme virtue because it is the guarantor of every other virtue." —Bergen Evans[7]

Courage or fortitude guarantees the other virtues. This is why it is such an important virtue to hone, my friend. How do you become fortitudinous? Begin by doing all your daily duties with discipline and diligence. If you are called upon for heroism, face that with courage as well. Most frequently, however, you will be faced with the mundane tasks of rising from bed each day, caring for the physical and emotional needs of your family and friends, caring for your health by eating and exercising appropriately, going to your job, training in your craft to be a better protector (if you are in a professional role), and preparing for that one day you may be called upon to stop violence or defend truth.

The Gregory Stevens Story

One man whom I interviewed, Gregory Stevens, patiently had served as a police officer for decades with no incident. He never needed to fire his weapon on the job, that is, until he did need to.

---

[7] FBB, pg. 175

Greg had trained for a lifetime for this one day, his moment of truth. Two would-be terrorists got out of a car at the public event where Greg was providing security. They were armed with rifles and were seeking to visit death and suffering upon the people. Greg, armed only with his sidearm, was able to neutralize both attackers by himself. Greg was awarded the Presidential Medal of Valor for his actions.[8]

How Does Officer Stevens' Story Apply to You?

How does Greg's story apply to you? Greg had trained for a lifetime without ever being called upon in such a manner. But do you know what he told me when I asked him why he thought he was able to be victorious on the battlefield that day? He said:

"I was diligent in my training. I never got complacent and I always knew the training would pay off."

He sought out opportunities to get more training than what was required; he went above and beyond—because that's what a warrior does. He knew that no matter how peaceful his career had been, it would take only one violent incident to end his career and/or life, not to mention the lives of others. So he trained; which brings us to another element of fortitude.

---

[8] https://www.dallasnews.com/news/politics/2016/05/16/garland-police-officer-who-stopped-isis-inspired-shooting-honored-with-medal-of-valor

Fortitude as the Cause of Training

Fortitude is required in order to prepare yourself to be able to face evil, even if you currently are not facing it. Fortitude is the ability to train for an event that may never occur, just in case. If you're a professional protector or a private citizen who arms himself (gun, knife, tactical pen, or any tool of self-protection) when you leave the house (or walk around in your own house), you've heard people say this: "Why do you carry weapons? Nothing is going to happen." Or how about this one: "Are you planning on being attacked? If not, why do you need to carry your gun?" If you are feeling snarky you could ask: "Do you own a fire extinguisher in your home?" "Yes I do." "Why? You planning on having your house burn down?" Let them think about that one for a while. "But won't preparing for violence make me paranoid?" To neutralize this nonsense, I shall quote Lt. Col. Dave Grossman:

"Preparation cures paranoia. It's denial that gets us killed."

However, you and I know the reason why you carry a tool to protect yourself and your loved ones: If a moment of truth like what happened to Officer Stevens visited you and you failed to arm yourself with the necessary tools and your loved ones died because of your failure, you couldn't live with the guilt. That is why you train for a lifetime, hoping the moment of truth never comes, but being prepared for it just in case. It is easy to make excuses to avoid training. It is easy to make excuses for failing to prepare for violence. All your excuses are valid until they are not. Interviewee Rory Miller once told me in a conversation:

> **"It is not morally superior to choose to be unprepared like MacGyver." —Rory Miller**

How true! How fortunate that Officer Stevens had the diligence and fortitude to train and prepare for his moment of truth rather than offer up excuses. Dozens of people could have been killed by those attackers if Officer Stevens had failed to prepare—if he lacked fortitude. Stop and consider this for a moment: How many people have died throughout history because a person or persons who were entrusted to be protectors failed to adequately prepare for violence? How many people have died because the protector got complacent, underestimated the enemy, or shirked their training (physical, emotional, mental, and spiritual). How many times did cowardice on the battlefield cost lives? This applies to you because how many times has personal cowardice cost you something in your life? Did it cost you a promotion at work, peace of mind, a date?

Were you fired from your job? Did someone die? As you can see, the lack of virtue is truly at the root of all unnecessary death and suffering. Don't misunderstand me. Bad things certainly can and do happen to good, virtuous people. It is also true that no matter how virtuous you are, an enemy could still victimize you in some way. If these things are true, then what chance do you have for preventing violence if you lack fortitude and courage? If you could still lose even when you have and exhibit the highest form of courage, then what will be your fate if you fail to practice this virtue at all? What will be the fate of those you are entrusted to protect?

Fortitude, Denial, and Consequences

Perhaps you don't like thinking too much on what I just said in the last paragraph. Better to just avoid thinking about it and deny that it exists, right? No. If you don't like thinking about the potential consequences of your behavior (or lack thereof), it's time to get some fortitude in your life because fortitude is the antidote to denial. Fortitude is the virtue that allows you to see reality for what it is. The truth hurts. It's why so many live in denial. Denial is not a luxury that you, as a warrior, can afford. Denial wasn't going to help Officer Stevens. Denial wasn't going to save Capt. Plumb. Denial won't help any soldier, officer, EP, security guard, bouncer, nurse, doctor, lawyer, parent, sibling, shop owner, coworker, mother, or father when violence comes to visit them—but fortitude just might. Strive for this virtue with all your tenacity and soak in all these dimensions I'm talking about and truly *be* virtuous. It takes fortitude to see reality for what it is, whether that means your school needs to fortify their entrances and update their security protocols, or realizing that the anger and bitterness inside you is killing you. Both these things take courage to admit and courage to create and work on a solution. Let me ask you: Did Officer Stevens require courage only in the moment of attack? No! Far from it. He had courage the whole way leading up to the attack, and during and after. If your courage lasts only momentarily, you will not follow through and persevere. The aftermath of violence requires its own courage, which leads us to another aspect of fortitude: resilience. Too many people think courage is merely a one-time heroic act. Not so! Fortitude is holistic; it is applied to and in all times: past, present, and future.

Fortitude as a Process

Capt. Charlie Plumb said during our interview: "Courage is a process." He said simply what I have taken many words to say. This is simple wisdom that could come only from experience. A man who was imprisoned with Capt. Plumb, Capt. Guy Gruters, said:

"Courage is fear that has said its prayers." What a quote. Courage being a process is such a vital takeaway that I want you to place it firmly inside your heart. If courage is a process, and not simply an act of heroism, that makes it accessible to all of us—to me, to you, and to everyone. You have the capacity for progressive, daily courage. Think to your own life: What slow, mundane processes must you go through each day? Does it not take courage to continually face them? Yes. Is not your virtue of fortitude forged over time, like a process? Yes, it is. Each day, with intentional action, you can acquire a little more, and a little more. Like the gradual trickle of a stream.

What is Fortitude?

Fortitude is courage, bravery, endurance, a process, action, doing your duty, embracing truth, resilience, consistency despite your fears, and forgiveness. Fortitude is the discipline to do what needs to be done based on an honest admission of reality. Fortitude is sacrifice. Let's face it, it is not easy living life like a protector. It is far easier to act entitled and cry and moan for others to serve you instead. The conundrum of wanting to be served should be painfully obvious: if everyone acted entitled and needed to be served, there would be no one to serve them. This would be the end of civilization and relationships as we know it. On the other hand, if everyone served one another, each of us would have a tremendous abundance in all aspects of life. If you have the heart of a protector or want to have it, sitting around acting entitled disgusts you to your very core. It is harder to go through life as a sacrificial, fortitudinous warrior, but you wouldn't have it any other way. I believe that the life of a warrior who lives virtuously with fortitude is a rich and blessed life. Along these lines, Lt. Col. Dave Grossman has one of my all-time favorite quotes:

> **"Sometimes the ultimate love is not to sacrifice your life, but to live a life of sacrifice." —Lt. Col. Dave Grossman**

It takes courage to lay down your life for your friends, but sometimes it takes even greater courage to live a life of sacrifice. What gives this life of sacrifice meaning and purpose? What motivates you? This is the virtue of love, the subject of Chapter 2.

In order to help you remember and utilize the seven virtues more effectively, I created seven corresponding postures for you to practice. When you want to remind yourself to be courageous and to live with fortitude, strike this pose while saying to yourself out loud, "I am courageous!"

Why do I recommend you do this?

You and I remember and retain more information when we are physically moving. We are biomechanical creatures and assigning a physical posture to each virtue will help to anchor them in your mind. This posture was chosen because you look like Superman ripping open your shirt to rush in and save the day. Superman faces his problems with courage and by performing this motion and posture, you will remind yourself to be courageous. There will be a posture at the end of each chapter. If you want to play a game, try to guess why I chose each posture before reading the description. Let's see how accurate your intuition is. Each of the postures were chosen not merely for their aesthetic appearances but also due to the physical, martial, fighting applications they each contain. Each of the seven postures contains a myriad of fighting and combat applications that I show my clients. If you want to discover what some of them are, subscribe to *The Anatomy of a Warrior Show*'s YouTube channel:

https://www.youtube.com/channel/UCB4Y_6Rwcgg1t6k2X-ZqDlg

Chapter 2: On Love

"Happy is he who dares to courageously defend what he loves." —Ovid[9]

The singer Haddaway once famously asked: "What is love?" This is a very important question to ask and one that we must explore due to the myriad of false and erroneous views that exist. "Love" is a word that (at least in the English language) we use to mean all manner of things, ranging from "I love lemonade" to saying "I love you" to your spouse. We clearly don't love the lemonade the way we love our spouse (at least I hope not). Using only one word, however, has led to much confusion on this topic. Let's define what we are talking about.

Protector Love

Love, the kind that is useful and necessary to being a good protector, is not the "I love lemonade" love. It is the self-sacrificial love—the love that places the needs of others over the needs of self. It takes a sacrificial love for you to be a protector because there exist far easier jobs. It is also far easier to be selfish and to seek your own gain at the expense of others. As a protector, you must

---

[9] FBB, pg. 541

wage war against this selfishness. The deepest parts of the heart are revealed only in love and suffering. This love can be manifested in acute acts of heroism or in the daily performance of a duty. The acute act of love is described in the Bible, John 15:13:

> **"Greater love hath no man than this; that a man lay down his life for his friends."**[10]

To die so that others may live is the ultimate expression of love. If you wish to take up the mantle of being a protector, this is something that you must reconcile and come to terms with in your own mind. Are you willing to lay down your life so that others can live? This introspection requires brutal honesty. Realize that comparatively few are called upon to such level of sacrifice, but it is something you should be prepared to do if you must. The mundane, daily struggle of life also requires consistent self-sacrifice. To continue to wake up each day, strap on your gear, and go out into the world to defend innocent people from the forces of darkness requires you to live a certain way. By definition, then, this choice precludes you from living another way, which means that "other way" you could have lived has been sacrificed for the warrior way.

---

[10]

https://www.biblegateway.com/passage/?search=John+15%3A13&version=KJV

Why do you do it? It's certainly not as safe for you to go out and face danger, but if you love others, you do it because it will make them safer.

Love as Service

A great many of the 120W spoke about empathy, compassion, and caring for their fellow human beings. Many more talked about service. To protect is to serve. You are rendering a service to yourself, your family, your community, and your country when you protect. This is true whether you are a Navy SEAL on a mission or a mother turning on the home alarm system before going to bed at night. Both of these are acts of service to others, your community, your nation, and your world. Once again, this means that no matter what your role or roles are in life, you have a part to play and can truly make a difference in the world. If you strive to acquire this virtue of love, you are doing your part. As with all virtues, love is a verb. It is action. Saying "I love you" when no actions reflect it is to lie or to delude yourself. Behavior reflects the inner content of your heart. Many of the 120W spoke about service, a dedication to service, and similar beliefs. How do you dedicate yourself to a life of service? One thing that helped me is realizing that no matter what you choose to do with your life, you are in the service business. You will either serve others or yourself. All decisions you make are on that spectrum somewhere. Sometimes you have win-wins where both parties are served. At other times you serve yourself at the expense of others. I would argue, however, that if you serve others, you are always serving yourself. Because in the ultimate sense, it is impossible to serve others without serving yourself.

"It is one of the beautiful compensations of life that no man can sincerely try to help another without helping himself." —Ralph Waldo Emerson[11]

To me, this makes service to others the obvious best choice, for it ensures perpetual win-wins. It ensures that you will also always be serving yourself. In one of life's great paradoxes, the greatest way to be selfish is to be unselfish. The best way to serve yourself is to serve others. I am amazed at how many times I must repeatedly learn this lesson. I don't fancy myself a stupid man by any means, but it seems I am in constant need of a reminder that if I really want to do well for myself, I should busy myself doing good for others. Can you relate to this? Why do I constantly need to keep my hand on the rudder to guide myself in the direction of service of others? Human nature. Love must be guided like a ship—it must be guided

---

[11] https://www.goodreads.com/quotes/29365-it-is-one-of-the-beautiful-compensations-of-life-that

towards the end of serving others. You must never take your hand off the rudder, lest the ship begin to turn in any direction at the whim of the chaos of the sea.

9/11 and Love

When most people heard about the planes being hijacked on 9/11, they said: "I'm glad I wasn't on that plane." What did all the protectors of our nation say? "I wish I had been on that plane. Maybe I could have made a difference." Where does such a sentiment come from? Love. What would make you want to be on a plane that was being hijacked instead of some other poor soul? The self-sacrificial love of a warrior.

Where does Love Proceed From?

Love ultimately flows from and resides in the heart. You and I are capable of this love—I believe it to be a free act of the will. It is important to remember that putting on a uniform and fighting bad guys does not necessarily mean you have love for your fellow man. Have you met anyone who wears a uniform who you could tell does not love people? Likewise, being unwilling to meet violence with violence does not necessarily mean you have love for your fellow man. Sometimes, true love requires us to meet unjust violence with violence so that innocent lives are protected. True love proceeds from your heart and requires purity of intention. Why do you protect? Take great care to truly foster within your heart a love for your fellow man. It will make your job much simpler and give your heart immense peace and tranquility. "But Alex, I'm a cop/soldier/EP, etc., and we fight evil, bad guys. They don't deserve to be loved!" To that, I say:

"Love means to love that which is unlovable, or it is no virtue at all." —G.K. Chesterton[12]

Okay, so I'll let G. K. Chesterton say it. Let me tell you a story from one of the interviewees, Michael Dorn, to illustrate this point of loving the unlovable.

The Michael Dorn Story

Michael Dorn was a cop in Georgia for years. He had always gone above and beyond, seeking the highest-quality training he could find. On two separate occasions, he faced 15-year-old males who pulled guns on him (one of them was also a special needs individual) and he did not shoot either one. In each case, the perpetrators dropped their weapons when Officer Dorn told them to. In both cases, he could have shot the young men who were

---

[12] FBB, pg. 539

presenting weapons as they were viable, deadly threats. But he didn't. He told me that he didn't shoot them ". . . because I did not need to shoot." Officer Dorn had trained and prepared so well that the young men could sense that if they chose to shoot at him, they were not going to win that gunfight. Hence, Michael Dorn's dedication to training saved these young men's lives.

Why is this an Example of Love?

While this story could equally serve as an example of the fortitude to train in Chapter 1, I am citing it here because I believe it takes an underlying love for your fellow man to commit to such a level of training in the first place. It takes a sincere love and value for human life to not shoot those two young men in a deadly situation—a genuine love and desire to keep people safe. Michael Dorn would have been justified in shooting both perpetrators but because he genuinely cares for his fellow man, he trained hard so that his skill was so precise that he did not need to shoot them. He saw it as his duty to protect all life, even the lives of the criminals. This does not mean he wouldn't have shot them if he needed to; it simply means that he prepared for violence so well that he was able to avoid shooting these two young men – his love compelled him to train hard which gave him options in the moments of violence he faced.

He truly saw it as his duty to not only protect himself, but to protect those young men from him and from themselves. This takes a deeper love. He loved what many would call "the unlovable", the criminals. Someone who lacked Michael Dorn's training would have been far more likely to shoot those two young men. Why? Because they wouldn't have had another option (at least, they would not have perceived that they had any other options in their own mind). Let love motivate you to train to acquire skill of heart, mind and body so that you have the choice to kill or not to kill if need be. There are many lessons to be learned from Michael Dorn's story – I recommend re-reading it and seeing what other lessons of virtue you can glean.

The Challenge of Love

This is the true challenge of love. As Chesterton rightly observed, you must love that which is unlovable. Many of the interviewees (especially the cops) talked about this. In police work, you see the underbelly of mankind every day. It is very easy to grow callous and become uncaring for the people you are serving. Interviewee Charles "Chip" Huth said that a protector must be compassionate, which he defined as "empathy with a strong desire to relieve human suffering." Well spoken. I would argue that one cannot have this strong desire without love.

How to Love the Unlovable?

How do you love that which is hard to love? Intentionally ask yourself the question: "Is there anything about this person, place, or thing that is good? Anything that is noble? Anything that is worthy of praise?" If that doesn't work, turn the question around and ask: "Is there anything I can gain from loving this person, place, or thing? What good can arise from me loving him/her/it/the situation?" Sometimes you love a person even when you know they will never love you back. Again, I am not referring to romantic love or feelings-based love, but self-sacrificing, altruistic love. Criminals may never love you back or love what you have done for him, but you must love them, and the innocents, enough to do your job.

"My People"

I submit to you that as a protector, if you can strive for this virtue of love and love the people you serve, even the criminals, your task will become far easier and lighter, and the burdens you carry less heavy. Interviewee and legendary police officer Gary Klugiewicz said that you should view all people as "your people." He would say of inmates or criminals he was dealing with: "these are my people."

He was quick to point out that just because they are your people, that doesn't mean you do not enforce the law. It doesn't mean you excuse their wrongdoing. But you do view them as "my people" because you have been tasked with protecting them and protecting society from them.

Insight from Interviewee, Jack Colwell

Interviewee and police officer Jack Colwell said: "When you look at people, see people." What a poignant reminder. Too often, I think police officers, soldiers, and civilians alike fail to see criminals, enemies, or citizens with different opinions as people. As a protector, dare to break this paradigm. Shift your focus over to the fact that they are human beings whose lives are valuable. Interviewee Jack Hoban says: "Life is the absolute value." (Jack wrote a great book entitled *The Ethical Warrior*[13], which I highly recommend for more wisdom on this point). If you do not believe life has this absolute value, love becomes quite difficult and atrocities are not far behind. History is replete with genocides and massacres that stemmed from a premise of "The enemy is not human" belief. This does not mean that while in war, you do not do what you must to protect yourself and comrades, but war is no excuse for atrocities

---

[13] https://www.amazon.com/Ethical-Warrior-Values-Morals-Service/dp/1475156685/ref=asap_bc?ie=UTF8

and if the reason you went to war was to exterminate your "non-human" enemy, you are the bad guy.

Gazing Into the Abyss

Friedrich Nietzsche wrote:

> **"And if you gaze long into an abyss, the abyss also gazes into you."**[14]

I believe that love is the antidote to the abyss. Love is what prevents a seasoned protector who has seen much bloodshed from descending into the abyss of despair, nihilism, callousness, and frigid roboticism. Taking on the task of protecting others does not mean you must burden yourself with all their cares and troubles. It simply means you protect them and do what is in your power to make them safe. A wise man once said: "You are responsible to people but not for them," meaning that you cannot control their behavior. You love them and do your best to protect them, but you must let go of the outcomes and whether or not they change their behavior.

---

[14] https://www.brainyquote.com/quotes/keywords/abyss.html

Loving People Enough to Let Go of Outcomes

I had to learn this lesson in my own personal life when I left the cult (if you jumped to this chapter, see the first exposition of the cult I left in Chapter 1, A Personal Story of Fortitude). At first, I struggled with the notion that other members could hear my story, see the evidence, and yet remain in the cult. How could they do this? I was very frustrated and upset at the time. Upon later reflection, I realized this was getting me down because I had anchored my happiness or emotions to the outcome of whether or not they would allow the evidence to persuade them to leave the cult. That was my mistake. Once I realized that I had served them and did my job as a protector by informing them of the nature of the cult, I began to feel better. The outcome is in their hands, and I understand that now. By continuing to stare into this "abyss," I would have harmed myself further. Love other people and yourself enough to protect them without becoming attached to the outcomes of their behaviors. Remember, if you take on another person or group of person's issues to the extent that they incapacitate you or cripple your ability (physical, emotional, psychological, and spiritual ability) to be an effective protector, you do them, yourself, your family and the community at large a disservice. They need you to be able to protect. You need you to be able to protect. True protector love appreciates this and sets up the appropriate boundaries to love your fellow men without allowing yourself to be incapacitated.

Love and Free Will

This brings us to a crucial discovery: Love respects the free will decisions of your fellow man. It doesn't mean you condone bad behavior or that you would recommend others repeat such bad behavior, but when you truly love someone you respect their free will. If you are an employer, respect the free will of your employees. It doesn't mean you let them do whatever they want, for real love also enforces rules and boundaries, but you never see them as lesser beings for the choices they've made. If you are a parent, respect the free will of your over-the-age-of-reason children. It doesn't mean you let them run the household, but act out of love when making decisions, instead of viewing them as lesser beings.

How Does this Apply to You?

What if you are not a cop? How does this apply to you as a civilian? Well, are you a parent? If you are a parent, you are a protector. You have been given a child to protect and raise well. Instilling in them the virtue of love and modeling it for them is a way of protecting them from evil, chaos, violence, and disaster later in life. How?

Because if they experience a healthy, self-sacrificing love from you, they will be more likely to love appropriately as adults. Love, the type of protector love we are discussing, is a free will choice. It is not a feeling, emotion, or passing fancy. It is a deep-rooted commitment and act of pure will that says: "I care about you enough to sacrifice for you." Love as a free will choice places it totally within your domain of control. Feelings are fleeting and cannot be controlled so easily. The will is yours to command if you so choose.

Selflessness

Another element of love is selflessness. Many of the 120W mentioned selflessness. Whence comes selflessness, and how can we more easily become selfless? Love. Focus on others first. My favorite philosophy professor at my Alma mater, the University of Akron, Joseph LiVecchi, taught me that:

"Love is to will the good of another for its own sake." — **Joseph LiVecchi**

It takes selflessness to will the good of another for its own sake. I am speaking of true altruism. Some have argued that such altruism does not exist. I disagree. Kyle Carpenter, the youngest living Medal of Honor recipient, threw himself on a live grenade to save his comrades[15]. He wasn't going to get much out of such a sacrifice except death. Yet he did it. He willed the good of his comrades above his own. That is true selflessness. Perhaps most importantly for you and me, when Carpenter was interviewed by David Letterman on *The Late Show*[16], Letterman asked if he threw himself on the grenade because of what was innate within him, or was it due to the training he received as a Marine? Kyle said that while he would like to think it was a little bit him, he gives full credit to the training he received as a Marine, or for being instilled with the proud history that goes with being a Marine. If Kyle can be trained to perform such acts of pure selflessness and love, so can you. Whether you are in the military or a private citizen, you can forge your own virtue so that you can demonstrate love under pressure.

True Self-Love

Another element of love that is completely misunderstood today is self-love. Self-love is a necessary element and component of love, but not in the way our consumer-driven media would have you believe. Interviewee Amanda Collins is a mother and rape survivor[17]. Her story is powerful, and she illustrates the true version of self-love—valuing your own life enough to fight back against an attacker.

---

[15] https://en.wikipedia.org/wiki/Kyle_Carpenter
[16] https://www.youtube.com/watch?v=VJJ1TXBY62c
[17] https://www.youtube.com/watch?v=1eSxaBEOx7c

You must understand that you have value. Interviewee and rape survivor Kimberly Corban agrees with Amanda Collins as well. Both women were attacked by men who stalked them on college campuses, and both agree that valuing their own lives and seeing themselves as valuable people helped to ensure that they survived not only the rapes, but the aftermath as well. Both have gone on to become Second Amendment advocates and positive voices for protecting women from violence.

How to Build Self-Esteem

How does one acquire a healthy self-esteem? One way to foster this healthy self-love is to believe you have a higher purpose. This is the subject of Chapter 6. While you don't allow self-love to consume you because this leads to selfishness, you must have a healthy perspective and understanding of how to love yourself as well. Real love in this sense is more of a duty. It is your duty to take care of your body, your spirit, and your mind. You love yourself enough to eat well, pray, feed your soul, study, and read to fill your mind with good things.

Charity

Another word that has been used to describe this type of love is charity. C.S. Lewis writes about charity in his book *The Four Loves*:

"Charity (*agápē*, Greek: ἀγάπη) is the love that exists regardless of changing circumstances. It is also called 'the God-love.'"[18]

If you base your love on things that change (looks, politics, opinions of the day, someone's ability to do something for you, and so on) it will be shaken or even destroyed when those things change. The real love of a warrior and protector, which will help you to successfully do your job is the love of charity. Charity is immovable, unchanging, everlasting, and pure. This is the type of love you must strive for as you walk the path of the warrior. How often have you seen people get divorced because their love was based on things that change rather than Lewis's *agápē* love? As examples, a man may leave his wife for a younger, sexier model. A woman may leave her husband because he is injured and can no longer work the way he used to. These examples illustrate what happens when you love someone based on accidental features (good looks and utility)

---

[18] https://en.wikipedia.org/wiki/The_Four_Loves#Agape.E2.80.94unconditional_.27God.27_love

rather than basing love on charity. Charity is the ultimate foundation of all love and good works. It serves as the bedrock and unchanging source from which all your love and good deeds can flow. You will be tested and tempted throughout your entire life to base your love on anything but charity. Charity is what allowed Capt. Plumb to forgive his torturers. Charity is what will afford you, as a protector, peace amid the chaos. When your foundation is unassailable, you can remain peaceful even during the most powerful storm.

Note on Religion

What religion—or lack thereof—you may possess should not matter when it comes to the love we are describing here. You do not have to belong to any particular religion to be charitable or to know that being charitable is a good thing. However, your foundational beliefs about God and the universe do play a role in whether or not you place value on being charitable. I challenge you to examine your own worldview to see if charity finds a coherent, satisfactory place within it. Where love comes from exceeds the scope of this book, but if you are curious, I would do some research to discover its origin.

Sheepdogs and Sheep

A popular notion in the protector community is that of the sheepdog and the sheep, made popular by Lt. Col. Dave Grossman. Rory Miller said that it is important to remember that you need the sheep, and the sheep need you. A good reminder. I have caught myself at times feeling superior to the sheep because "I'm the sheepdog." This is a bad feeling and an incorrect notion to have. Being a warrior does not make me superior to those who are not. I might be a superior fighter compared to some of them, but as a human being, I am no greater than they are. Elitism does not lead to love—it leads to smugness and condescension, which are poor incubators for love. As a fellow sheepdog, do you not do what you do in order to serve and protect the sheep? My Top Tier client and good friend Lawrence Halmasy said in a discussion we were having on this very topic:

"If we do not make the time for our family, then what is the point of being a protector?"

Protection for the sake of protection is meaningless. It must go deeper than that. Protection because you love the sheep is deep and satisfactory. You are a sheepdog, but you need the sheep as much as the sheep need you. The sheep give you purpose. Never forget that.

Empathy

Another aspect of love that many of the 120W mentioned was empathy. The dictionary defines empathy as "the ability to understand and share the feelings of another." Being able to understand the feelings of others can help to make them more human in your mind. This is a very important thing. However, sharing in the feelings of others can be detrimental and unproductive. If you do attempt to share in their feelings, be cautious, for another element of being a good protector is being able to prudently discern reality and make effective judgments for how to act (the subject of Chapter 5). Too much feeling the way the criminal, spouse, victim, child, friend, feels may cloud your judgment, which oftentimes is actually the opposite of what that person needs. Love gives a person what they need, not necessarily what they want.

The Dr. Sudip Bose Story - The Man Who Treated Saddam Hussein

To illustrate this point, I will tell you the story of interviewee Dr. Sudip Bose who served as a field medic in the U.S. Army. He was one of the longest-serving medics since World War II. As fate would have it, he was chosen to be the man who treated Saddam Hussein after the United States captured him on December 13th, 2003. It would have been very easy to let his personal feelings get in the way of doing his job but Dr. Bose did not allow that. He faithfully carried out his duty. This is a form of protector love because once Saddam was caught, and was no longer a viable threat, the objective shifted from that of capturing him to medically treating and examining him. By focusing on the task at hand, Dr. Bose was able to perform his duty and aid the captured Saddam Hussein.

Compartmentalization

Dr. Bose also told me a story of when he was trying to fix up a soldier on the battlefield, and how he needed to be able to compartmentalize things appropriately. To share in too many feelings of the injured soldier ("Is this soldier going to die? Is he leaving a wife and children behind?") is not what that soldier needed—he needed a good medic to fix him. Dr. Bose even went so far as to say you almost have to ignore those feelings and simply focus on the task at hand. This is true sacrifice and love. Why? Because selfishly, it is more natural and easier to start feeling what the wounded soldier feels. We tend to project and put ourselves in the other person's situation. This is what makes certain movies and works of art so powerful. But you, as a protector, know that if you truly love your fellow man, you will put aside your feelings and get busy fixing and serving others. Did not our first responders on 9/11 demonstrate this very thing? Yes. They loved the injured and crying civilians enough to forgo sharing in their grief—in order to continue saving more lives. That is true self-sacrifice and denial. This is a powerful element of love that, I feel, does not get the attention it deserves. Our first responders do not receive enough credit for the jobs they do. I have a cousin and several friends who are firefighters and paramedics, and the stories they tell me are heartbreaking. Frequently they approach a scene, not knowing yet if it is safe and secure, but knowing that a drug overdose victim needs to be resuscitated. Family could be around helping or making the situation worse. Babies could be crying. It is awful. But thinking about the feelings of the victims and their families isn't going to help them— doing their jobs and administering the NARCAN will. Perhaps that is the distinction: Have empathy, but know when and how to shut it off and turn it on. After 9/11, I'm sure many of those first responders (those who survived) went home and wept bitterly. Love knows all proper boundaries and all appropriate timing. There is a time for grief, but it isn't in the middle of battle. There is a time for empathy but it isn't while you are trying to surgically remove a bullet from someone. If your child goes missing, now isn't the time for falling to the ground like a basket case—now is the time to search and find your child. Putting yourself in the shoes of the parents of a kidnapped child as a detective is helpful when you are not on a case. Putting yourself in their shoes may be beneficial for a criminal profiler to discover a vital piece of information that could lead to the arrest of the perpetrator and the return of the child. But taking on all the feelings of the parents is not helpful in the heat of trying to solve the crime. During the investigation, the parents don't need you to empathize, they need you to focus, do your job, and find their child. This is a very tough thing to do and often I feel protectors who compartmentalize are sometimes seen as callous and unfeeling by those who do not understand. A calculated exterior does not mean that, interiorly, there is no love. In fact, quite the opposite can be true. I would argue that oftentimes that callousness comes from a place of love. They love the victim enough to put aside their desire to feel, and instead focus on the task at hand. Empathy during a quiet moment of reflection is important and good for a protector. No matter how much of a bulletproof machine you think you are, you are mortal—mere flesh and bone like anyone else. It's okay to empathize—just know when it is appropriate to do so, and know your own personal limits as to how far you can go.

Enemies of Love

Hubris and pride are powerful enemies that will thwart your attempts to become virtuously loving. Interviewee Ken Murray said:

"Hubris shuts people down from being compassionate."
A very insightful remark. Pride does this because pride is excessive self-love. As we've already seen, too much self-love takes the focus away from serving others and becomes self-serving. Too much focus on the self begins to isolate you internally from your fellow man, which leads you to scoff at his problems. This will degrade your compassion. Guard against the enemy of pride, my friend. There is another enemy you must guard against. It has been said that the opposite of love is indifference. Guard against this, my friend! It is not strength to become numb to the cares and plights of your fellow man. I believe it is actually cowardice of the highest order. It is also selfish. Indifference can lead to complacency, which leads to errors, oversights, and mistakes that could cost you or another person their life. It is my opinion that, in the routine of daily life, indifference is surely the cause of many divorces, depression,

lack of fulfillment in work, and other troubles. Guard against this enemy with all your strength by actively loving and being charitable. Remember what Chesterton said: "love the unlovable."

Fear

Fear is another powerful enemy that you must protect yourself from as well. In Steven Pressfield's iconic book *Gates of Fire*[19], he writes of the Spartans' Battle of Thermopylae against the Persians. In it, the older warriors ask the young Spartan soldiers what the opposite of fear is. It is revealed to them that the opposite of fear is love.

"Greater is he who acts from love than he who acts from fear." —Simeon Ben Eleazar[20]

The antidote to fear is love. Love is a limitless source that can overcome any fear if you believe it can and take the necessary actions to fight back against fear. Whether you fear a home invasion, the stock market collapsing, or a natural disaster, love is what will motivate you to prepare for and do battle against what you fear—even to the loss of your own life if need be.

---

[19] https://www.amazon.com/dp/B000NJL7QO/ref=dp-kindle-redirect?_encoding=UTF8&btkr=1
[20] FBB, pg. 539

How to Become Unconquerable

If you can truly love the unlovable, you become an unstoppable force. What can slander, bigotry, hatred, and indifference do when faced with calm, steady love? Nothing. They are defeated. This is quite a difficult thing to master, and I am by no means a master of it yet. However, it is a noble goal. If you can love the unlovable, your spirit becomes unconquerable. I do not mean that you tolerate evil men or behavior. I do not mean that you do not take swift, violent action when necessary to protect. I mean that when your ultimate, driving motive for all your actions and behavior becomes love, you become unconquerable in spirit and in mind. If you can come to love even your own suffering, there is no enemy that can defeat you. This is quite a challenging task, but it is the true path to freedom and perfection. St. Augustine said, "Love and do as thou wilt." If you admonish someone, do it out of love. If you grieve with someone, grieve out of love. If you compete to win a tournament, do it out of love. In other words, if love of others before yourself is the prime motivating factor, you are far less likely to behave inappropriately. This type of love is purity of intention, or altruistic motives. But obviously, you need skill sets to carry out certain tasks. I can act out of as much love as I want, but I am not going to be able to carve

Michelangelo's statue, *David*, out of marble—I lack the skill. But my motives can be pure, and this is the type of love I am referring to. This type of motive makes you unconquerable as a protector because nothing that anyone throws at you can shake your foundation and the source of where your love comes from.

Final Thoughts on Love

Real love is rooted in a strong moral conviction—in the belief of an ultimate standard of good and evil, right and wrong. For if such a standard did not exist, how would we know the boundaries of love, or any other virtue for that matter? This standard has been called justice, and that brings us to chapter 3.

In order to help you remember and utilize the seven virtues more effectively, I created seven corresponding postures for you to practice. When you want to remind yourself to be loving, strike this pose while saying to yourself out loud, "I am loving!"

Why do I recommend you do this?

You and I remember and retain more information when we are physically moving. We are biomechanical creatures and assigning a physical posture to each virtue will help to anchor them in your mind. This posture was chosen because you look like you are giving yourself a hug. While I designed these postures to be able to be done alone, giving your spouse or loved ones a hug and reminding yourself to be loving is a great idea too. Don't mind the scowl I'm giving – you can strike this pose with a smile. There will be a posture at the end of each chapter. If you want to play a game, try to guess why I chose each posture before reading the description. Let's see how accurate your intuition is. Each of the postures were chosen not merely for their aesthetic appearances but also due to the physical, martial, fighting applications they contain. Hidden within the seven postures are a myriad of fighting and combat applications that I show to my clients. If you want to discover what some of them are, subscribe to *The Anatomy of a Warrior Show*'s

YouTube channel:

https://www.youtube.com/channel/UCB4Y_6Rwcgg1t6k2X-ZqDlg

Chapter 3: On Justice

"Justice is a certain rectitude of mind whereby a man does what he ought to do in the circumstances confronting him." —St. Thomas Aquinas[21]

St. Thomas sums up justice quite well. Appropriate action in a given circumstance equals justice. Circumstances vary and call for various responses, and truly wise is the person able to accurately distinguish what needs to be done and who then takes action on it. Knowing the right thing to do plus doing that thing equals justice. The opposite is also true: Knowing what is evil and preventing it—or putting a stop to it—is also justice.

How to Make Use of Justice?

In order for justice to be of any use to you, you must possess fortitude. Simply knowing the right thing is not enough. Correct knowledge is a good place to start, but for it to be of any use to you and to others, it must be courageously acted upon. How to know what is appropriate for any situation will be discussed in chapter 5, On Prudence.

---

[21] FBB, pg. 462

The Foundation of Justice

You can also see how justice must have love as its foundation. For love is the ultimate foundation of putting all the virtues into practice. Why? Because love is the ultimate motivator. Justice in and of itself may not motivate you, but love surely will. Likewise, fortitude for its own sake is rarely motivating. But if you heart is filled with love, you can be fortitudinous. Likewise, knowledge of what is right and wrong is rarely the determining factor behind the motivation of your behavior. You can think of countless situations where you knew a thing was wrong but did it anyway. You can also think of many examples where you knew what was right, but failed to do it. What we love is the ultimate motivator, so your first task is to love good things, healthy things that will not damage, corrupt, or stain your soul, mind, and body.

Right vs. Wrong

If you strive for the previous two virtues of fortitude and love, you will be far more likely to live by our third virtue of protectors: justice. A great many of the 120W talked about how it is essential for a protector to have a very well-developed sense of right and wrong. Justice is what ensures that we protect in the correct manner and at the appropriate time. For example, shooting an armed home invader who seeks to murder you is a just action. Preemptively shooting a person because you didn't like the glance they gave you is not. Crude and simple examples, but they illustrate the point that even though your behavior was exactly the same (i.e., shooting someone) the moral status changed from just to unjust based on the context, motives and surrounding circumstances.

No Legal Claims

Note that I am speaking of justice and injustice, not legal and illegal. This chapter is making absolutely zero legal claims in any way, shape, or form. A just action may be illegal. A legal action may be unjust. The 120W did not speak to me—nor were they asked for counsel or advice—about the legality of certain actions, such as when shooting a home invader is legally justified. The justice or injustice, legality or illegality, all vary depending upon circumstances, context, intent, abilities, nature of threats, laws (always subject to change), and other factors. If you want to learn more about the legal aspects of self-defense and personal protection, I recommend interviewee Massad Ayoob's books and articles.[22]

---

[22] http://massadayoobgroup.com/

A Sense of Justice

Perhaps more important than a simple knowledge of right and wrong is the deep rooted sense of justice you should strive to have as a protector. Most of the interviewees I spoke with had a burning passion to make the world a better place by keeping innocent people safe from violence. Why? Because it genuinely lights a fire inside them when they hear of an innocent person being victimized by violence. Hearing about innocent people being victimized elicits an enormously deep and profound thought and feeling in me that, "What happened to that person was wrong. It isn't right and I hope the criminal gets justice."

How Can You Develop Justice?

How can you develop this virtue of justice? Several of the 120W spoke of the importance of parenting and of having at least one good role model as a young person who was a man or woman of justice. The importance of guarding who and what has influence over your children cannot be overstated. The people they interact with, the media they consume, your example, are all crucial elements in developing the virtue of justice within your children. The best way mankind has ever found in training up virtuous individuals is if you, their parent, live virtuously. If you are already an adult, and those options have passed you by, one avenue that might prove useful is if you challenge your underlying worldview.

What Do You Believe?

You see, the interviewees are outraged at a woman being raped because they believe it is wrong. It would stand to reason, then, that if they didn't believe raping women was wrong, they wouldn't be outraged. Why do they believe raping women is wrong? Many of them may not have a succinct answer for that question. The "why" questions are very deep and can take time to answer. I submit the same question to you: Why do you believe that raping women is wrong? Substitute "raping women" for any other action or behavior that triggers your sense of justice. Why do you believe that ___ is wrong? Why do you believe that ___ is right? These types of "why" questions cannot be answered without delving into the realms of theology and religion, as they are matters of fundamental worldviews and beliefs. Theology and religion exceed the scope of this book, but you should be aware that these fundamental worldviews will greatly shape your ideas about justice. Your beliefs about justice inform your behavior and actions relating to that belief. I challenge you to examine your foundational beliefs about right and wrong, good and evil, and so on. Whatever your core beliefs, they are worth examining—you may be surprised at what you find.

Morality vs. Immorality

Another word some of the 120W used to describe this virtue is morality. What is morally permissible? How can you tell? These are questions philosophers and thinkers have asked for thousands of years. In your search, it may be helpful to note the difference between ontology and epistemology. Ontology deals with the nature of being, and epistemology deals with how we know things. Ontology is being as such; epistemology is how we know being as such. Let me give you some examples in the form of questions. "Is abortion moral or immoral?" That is an ontological question. I am asking what the ultimate truth of that claim is. "How do we know that abortion is moral or immoral?" Is an epistemological question. It doesn't deal with the ultimate truth value of the claim, but rather with how we know or how did we come to learn the ultimate truth value of that claim. I encourage you to ask these questions too, and to ask why you came to the conclusions you reached. It is a difficult exercise, and you may find yourself wondering if the core beliefs you have always held are true.

Truth and Reality

"The presupposition of Western Civilization is that the truth is the best defense against suffering."—Jordan Peterson[23]

I absolutely love this quote by Professor Jordan Peterson of the University of Toronto. Let it resonate deep into your mind and heart. I firmly agree with his statement. As a protector, you must walk in truth. Why? Because the truth is a synonym for "reality." How are you supposed to protect anyone or anything if you cannot perceive reality or refuse to acknowledge it for what it is? Lt. Col. Dave Grossman talks about "denial" as something that is bad for protectors to engage in. Denial of what? Of reality! Of the truth!

"Truth is the most fundamental component of justice."
—Interviewee Sid Heal

Of course, it helps if you believe in the existence of truth: A truth that transcends your own limited subjectivity—an external referent to which you and I can appeal and say: "This thing is not true, and that thing is true." It is not necessary to believe in a transcendent truth in order to protect people from violence, but it sure does help. It also gives a higher purpose and meaning to what you are doing, but this

---

[23] https://www.youtube.com/watch?v=p4obxH2vSms

element will be discussed more in Chapter 6, On Faith. Accepting the truth is precisely what allows you to solve problems. I want you to imagine you are at work right now, doing your normal routine. What problems are you faced with at work? Mull a few of them over in your mind. Now ask yourself: "Do I want solutions to these problems? Or do I only pretend to want solutions to these problems?" Or worse, do you pretend that your problems do not even exist at all? Ignorance will not save you from violence, and ignorance will not protect your loved ones from violence either. You and I do this all the time in our personal lives, and businesses do it all the time too—fixing fake problems, ignoring real problems, denying any problems exist at all, because we are unwilling to honestly confront and tackle our real issues.

Honesty

This brings us to another element of justice, which is honesty. Because you are committed to living a life in the service of the truth, you must then be honest with yourself and others. What problems do you really have? Where could an attacker truly exploit your school, house of worship, business, home, or other locations? What does your child really need from you as their parent? What does your spouse really want and need out of you to make your marriage better? A protector strives to be honest enough to face the truth and reality head on. All the interviewees talked about being honest about what reality is. In a violent situation, you must be honest about what is happening. Honesty is the antidote to denial. As a protector, you must deal with reality head on to solve the problem or neutralize the threat. The aftermath is the time for asking past or future questions such as: "Why did this person attack me? What could I have done differently to prevent it?" These are all good questions to ask, which themselves require you to have the honesty to admit the truth. If you lie and say: "I have no idea why I was attacked and don't care to know," you will not be able to find solutions. Imagine an executive protection agency that has a very powerful client assassinated. Then imagine if, after the incident, the top leadership says: "You know, we aren't going to study what went wrong here. We're just going to pretend that this never happened." Would you want to hire such a firm to protect you and your family?

Self-Honesty

Many of the interviewees talked about telling the truth and having self-honesty. Telling the truth is hard sometimes. Doing what is right can be difficult when no one else agrees with you. Doing the right thing despite peer pressure to do otherwise can be challenging.

Doing the right thing even when nobody's watching can be just as challenging. I faced this a great deal when writing this book. I am my own small business owner, so there is no one to tell me that I have to do anything. Some days when I was supposed to be working on this book, I shirked my duty and did something else. Oh, I always had a good excuse for not doing the work (something I'm sure you cannot relate to at all). Ironically, working on this project has helped me to honestly face my own issues with more honesty. As they say in 12-step programs, the first is admitting you have a problem. What does it take to admit you need help? Honesty. The cold, hard truth is that many of us lack this self-honesty. We may tell the truth to others, but we lie to ourselves all the time. You must strive to break free from this bad habit. If honesty is a warrior virtue the opposite of that is lying. Strive as best you can to eliminate all lying from your life, even the small ones that you think don't matter. They absolutely do matter. Rome wasn't built or destroyed in one day. Both were gradual processes. Even small lies tear at the very foundation of your character and cause it to become weaker. The Bible has a great verse about this very thing:

> **"He that is faithful in that which is least, is faithful also in that which is greater: and he that is unjust in that**

which is little, is unjust also in that which is greater." —

Luke 16:10[24]

What a perfect verse! It is talking about exactly what we are talking about—justice. Do not therefore deceive yourself, my friend, that telling small lies is helpful. It erodes your character. The standard isn't: "Hurray! I wasn't caught!" The standard is the truth. If you will lie about seemingly inconsequential things, what will you do when tremendous consequences are at stake? If you will lie about things that have little to no bearing on your job, income, self-image, reputation, and so on, what will you say or do when those things are on the line?

Building Trust

Here is perhaps the biggest, most practical reason why you must tell the truth to others and to yourself as a protector: Telling the truth and acting upon it builds trust with your spouse, coworkers, teammates, partners, employers, employees, children, parents, and fellow soldiers and officers. Only telling the truth and living it out can build trust. Lies do the exact opposite! If you are in the professional protector realm already, how many incidents can you think of where you caught someone in a lie and it caused you to doubt the person

---

[24] http://biblehub.com/luke/16-10.htm

or eroded your trust in them? Have you seen people get fired for lack of honesty? Have you seen lies lead to far worse consequences that could have been avoided if the person had simply told the truth from the outset? I'm sure we could fill a volume of thousands of pages listing them all.

Integrity

Telling the truth and acting it out has a simpler word that many of the 120W mentioned: integrity. Most defined integrity as saying and doing the right thing. What you say matches what you do and vice-versa. Integrity is from the Latin *integritas*[25], meaning whole, unified, or undivided. An integer in mathematics is a whole number. If you really think about it, this means that if you lack integrity, you are a divided person, a man at war with himself. And you know how well a house divided against itself stands, right? Integrity is often talked about in buildings to mean stable, strong, sound, and firmly grounded or foundationally steady. As a protector, you need this steely self-assurance that can only come from having a stable platform. In judo, for example, your goal and the opponent's goal is to off-balance each other to be able to throw or knock the other

---

[25]

https://www.google.com/search?q=etymology+of+the+word+integrity&rlz=1
C1GGRV_enUS748US748&oq=Etymology+of+the+word+integ&aqs=chro
me.1.69i57j0l5.10164j0j4&sourceid=chrome&ie=UTF-8

over. You must destroy the integrity of your opponent's base. You must destroy his structure. Integrity is the very structure of your character.

Bottom Line

The bottom line is this: If you want people to trust you, they must perceive you to be a person of integrity. If you truly have no integrity but have just been able to fool someone into thinking so, enjoy the ride while you can, because once you are discovered for a fraud, you will never regain their trust. This is exactly what I experienced when I found out that the claims my former martial arts instructor made were false. I had known him for 12 years. I trusted him. When I discovered that his claims were false, it destroyed the relationship. Why? Because I couldn't trust him anymore. If he lied about his background, what else was he lying about? Why did he lie in the first place? It was a bitterly hard pill to swallow, but it is a lesson I am very glad I learned. My ability to perceive reality is now sharpened by that experience, which will enable me to be a better protector. Realizing I was in a cult was a watershed moment for me. It taught me very powerfully what happens when you do not ask questions, don't do your due diligence in researching, and do not exercise caution in whom you trust. What was your watershed moment when it comes to honesty and integrity? What lesson did you learn? Were you ever betrayed and lied to? How did that make you feel? I'm guessing not well. As a protector, it is your duty to protect others from having to experience that, so make yourself an honest and integral person so that you are never the cause of that pain in another person's life.

Justice and Freedom

"Every man who expresses an honest thought is a soldier in the army of intellectual liberty." —Robert G. Ingersoll[26]

This quote by Ingersoll is how I hope you choose to view truth telling and honest living. You ensure the freedom, liberty, and security of other people by speaking the truth. It is the greatest antidote to human suffering ever discovered. As a protector, you are about finding solutions to problems and minimizing death and suffering, so it stands to reason that you should be of the truth and integrity—it is simply the most pragmatic way to achieve your goals. Living virtuously provides you with personal freedom. Your personal freedom bleeds out into your relationships with others, which hopefully inspires them to desire to partake in your freedom. Justice

---

[26] FBB, pg. 407

in particular ensures order and right conduct. Only by living according to true justice can you remain free from tyranny—both from external and internal threats. Justice is the barometer to judge yourself by. The more harshly and rigorously you hold yourself to the standard of justice, the more peace and freedom of the mind, soul, and will you experience. This is crucial for a protector because it provides you with the foundation you need to make sound judgments about yourself and external reality (people, places, and things). This thought will be expanded upon in Chapter 5, On Prudence.

Honor

Another element of justice that many of the 120W discussed is to be a person of honor. How does one become honorable? By being truthful. Honor is often thought of as a title like King, Queen, or having some celebrity or high social standing. They have great "honor" in society and the eyes of the world. This isn't the honor of a protector. Protectors know that honor is something you earn for yourself by being truthful and virtuous. If you live according to the truth and strive for and live with virtue, you will develop a strong and highly esteemed character. Your character, who you are, is what makes you honorable or not. You character is what makes you worthy of being honored by others. The cult leader gave himself many titles, names, and dignities, but he lacked honor. Why? Because he is a pathological liar and a fraud. No number of titles can bestow honor upon him because it isn't something anyone can bestow upon you. You cannot even "bestow" it upon yourself, apart from doing the work that earns it. Isn't that the problem with justice and all the other virtues in this book? None of them can simply be pronounced over you and voilà, you have those virtues! No. You must earn them on the battlefield of life and forge them in the crucible of adversity.

"Loyalty, trust, and honor are fragile. One instant can destroy them. Interestingly, they grow when given away." —Interviewee Sid Heal

Adversity

Adversity is why we marvel at heroic acts of virtue. Adversity and man's free will to choose to battle against it is why stories of heroic virtue inspire us so much—tales of survival and sacrifice that still the heart and shake the spirit. This is why fictional tales—such as J.R.R. Tolkien's *The Lord of the Rings*, which is still widely read even to this day, some 60+ years after publication. It is because the deeds of heroism, valor, and virtue in Tolkien's works inspire us. If fiction can have such a powerful effect, what could your good example do for someone else? What if someone looked at your virtuous deeds, small or great, and said: "Wow. That makes me want to strive for something greater." To have done this even for one person is to have succeeded as a protector.

> **"The shortest and surest way to live with honor in the world, is to be in reality what we would appear to be; all human virtues increase and strengthen themselves by the practice and experience of them." —Socrates**[27]

What a truly fantastic quote by Socrates. Be in reality what you would appear to be. Do you see this in business, where some people and companies attempt to look one way while they secretly live another way? This isn't the path of the warrior! The warrior has the courage, honesty, and integrity to admit who he is, what he is, where he is and why he is. Personally, I am weary of all the charlatans and scammers in the business world desperate to pick your pocket when they don't even have the decency to practice what they preach. It infuriates me and triggers my sense of justice because they are lying and deceiving people out of their hard-earned money. If you share this feeling, you are being a protector. You do not wish to see others defrauded of what they worked so

---

[27] FBB, pg. 410

hard to earn. It is unjust and it stirs up righteous indignation in my soul.

Justice Summarized

Justice is a broad, all-encompassing term to cover others such as integrity, honesty, righteousness, truthfulness, and trustworthiness. Justice is able to be enacted by protectors who can perceive reality accurately and who have the courage to face it head on. There is another virtue, however, that you must possess in order to perceive reality accurately, which also serves to temper your character lest you become arrogant in your pursuit of justice. This virtue is truly lacking in our world today, especially among those who possess high levels of skill and knowledge. A real warrior tempers himself by striving for our next virtue, that of humility.

In order to help you remember and utilize the seven virtues more effectively, I created seven corresponding postures for you to practice.

Why do I recommend you do this?

You and I remember and retain more information when we are physically moving. We are biomechanical creatures and assigning a physical posture to each virtue will help to anchor them in your mind. This posture was chosen because you look like you are balancing the scales of Lady Justice. You can do any variation of right and left arm so long as you feel like you are balancing the scales of justice. Strike this pose and say out loud, "I am just!" There will be a posture at the end of each chapter. If you want to play a game, try to guess why I chose each posture before reading the description. Let's see how accurate your intuition is. Each of the postures were chosen not merely for their aesthetic appearances but also due to the physical, martial, fighting applications they contain. Hidden within the seven postures are a myriad of fighting and combat applications that I show to my clients. If you want to discover what some of them are, subscribe to *The Anatomy of a*

Warrior Show's YouTube channel.

https://www.youtube.com/channel/UCB4Y_6Rwcgg1t6k2X-ZqDlg

Chapter 4: On Humility

"The wise person possesses humility. He knows that his small island of knowledge is surrounded by a vast sea of the unknown." —Harold C. Chase[28]

Be the Perpetual Student

One of the most important elements to being a successful protector, according to the 120W, is to constantly study and learn more about how to protect people—to be the consummate and perennial student for your entire life. "Always keep learning," and "Never think you know it all." Learning, in and of itself, is not a virtue. But there is a virtue underlying one's ability to be a perpetual student: humility. If you think you know it all, you have a profound lack of humility. This know-it-all attitude can lead you to avoid listening to someone else's ideas. It can cause you to become complacent and fall into a rut of not updating and upgrading your tactics, training, technology, and virtue. A protector never discounts the experience and knowledge of another. This does not mean that someone else's opinion is meritorious simply by virtue of it being a different opinion. It takes right judgment to be able to discern which opinions correspond to

---

[28] FBB, pg. 422

reality and which do not (a subject for Chapter 5) but if you lack humility, you will never consider any other input, because what could they possibly tell you that you don't already know? This attitude is to be purged and guarded against most vigorously if you want to become a better protector. Of all virtues, humility is perhaps the one you must cultivate most intently. Why? Because I believe that nothing is easier than to esteem yourself and your own deeds too highly. I am continually amazed at how quickly I attribute good things to myself and make excuses for the bad things. Can you relate?

The Temptation of Knowledge

As you read this book and continue to learn and study about the virtues of protectors, be watchful over your heart. For the more knowledge you acquire, the more you are tempted to become less humble. Many of the most insufferable, arrogant people are those who actually do have a great wealth of knowledge and skill. The more you learn, the more you must actively and intentionally strive to remain humble.

How can you accomplish this?

I have found that meditating on reality is helpful. If you employ the previously discussed virtue of honesty and reflect long enough on your own shortcomings, you should be sufficiently humbled. Your self-analysis should show you many areas of improvement. However, there is another, perhaps even more powerful tactic (if one can call it that) that you can use. C.S. Lewis once said:

"He [a man] will not be thinking about humility: he will not be thinking about himself at all."[29]

Unlike the other virtues, which can be enhanced by intently focusing on them and doing them, if one is constantly focused on "being more humble" it can actually retard the process. Why? Because you end up focusing on yourself. The whole process of intentionally focusing on acquiring more virtue can lead to an overinflated sense of righteousness and grandeur. What is to be done to rectify this dilemma? Turn your focus outward, toward selfless service to others. This will take your mind off yourself. This is why humility is a most precious virtue and why humility is vital to your success as a protector. Humility is the safeguard against falling in love with your own greatness. Be great, do great things, but also never allow your ego to become overinflated due to your greatness.

Ways to be Humble

---

[29] http://www.bloggingtheologically.com/2015/12/11/what-cs-lewis-wrote-is-better-than-what-he-didnt/

If you are a police officer, a small thing could be saying hello with a smile to the members of the community you serve, instead of walking past them with smugness and a feeling of moral superiority simply because you wear a badge and uniform. Do not forget you were once an ordinary citizen, just like them. For a truly humble officer, smiling and appreciating where you came from isn't difficult. The prideful officer may wake up one day realizing he is lording his authority over the citizens he swore an oath to protect. Pride brings with it resentment, and humility brings respect and admiration. For my professional protectors, humility is perhaps the greatest tool at your disposal to winning the trust and affection of the people you serve. When the people know that you could have lorded authority over them but you exercised restraint, stayed calm, and treated them with dignity, they are far more likely to respect you, and may even start supporting you in your task.

Know Your People

Interviewee and police officer Gordon Graham said that one of the most vital factors to being a good protector is to know the people in the community you want to protect. To actively know them. What virtue will enable you to get to know people more effectively? Humility. Getting to know someone properly requires that you genuinely care about who they are and what they have to say. Pride can prevent this. Humility is the antidote. Do not make the mistake of thinking humility applies only to protectors in the professional realm. This applies to you: the mother, the father, the business owner, the nurse, the lawyer, the dentist, the entrepreneur, the university professor, the employee, etc. Get to know your people in all your various communities—work, family, neighbors, and so on. Getting to know them will humanize them and make you more sympathetic to their problems. It also forces you to be interested in someone other than yourself.

Humility as a Preserving Agent

What greater way exists to preserve your marriage than fostering true humility? Imagine being genuinely concerned and preoccupied with serving your spouse first, instead of first thinking of what they can do for you. What would that do for your marriage? How would your children, coworkers, and relatives respond if you genuinely put this practice of humble service into action? It could revolutionize your life and your relationships. If you are in the professional protector realm and you hold a position of leadership, how do you think your team would respond to you genuinely being concerned for them? If you invested the time to get to know your teammates, co-workers and staff, how would that improve your ability to operate and protect people? Humility preserves unity and open communication by creating an environment where everyone can share their honest thoughts. It does this because you become actually interested in other people.

The Problems of Pride and Selfishness

A problem we see quite rampant in society today is the profound selfishness of it. Businesses compete instead of helping each other. Marriages fall apart because both parties only want to take from someone and not give to someone. We consume possessions and vacations past the point of what we can afford and then wonder why our lives are miserable. Humility is the antidote to this. C.S. Lewis wrote:

> **"If anyone would like to acquire humility, I can, I think, tell him the first step. The first step is to realize that one is proud."[30]**

As with all things, the first step is admitting you have a problem and need help. "Hi, my name is Alex Lanshe, and I am full of pride." Only when you honestly admit this can you set about forging the virtue of humility deep within your heart.

---

[30] http://www.bloggingtheologically.com/2015/12/11/what-cs-lewis-wrote-is-better-than-what-he-didnt/

Faux Humility

One thing you must take great caution against is the desire to appear humble before other people. This is the opposite of true humility, and in fact stems from pride. The same is true of all the virtues mentioned in this book. If you are pursuing any of them so that you may appear before others to be those things, you have a flawed intention and ironically move yourself further away from acquiring that virtue. I battle against this constantly in my own life. The desire to be esteemed, loved, and respected by others can greatly poison humility when it overflows its natural boundary. It is natural to want others to see you as virtuous, but do not allow this to become your primary motivation. Strive to drive it ever further down your priority list until it vanishes from sight and thought. One way to aid in this quest is to strive to love truth for its own sake. I wrote in one of my blogs: "Truth is its own reward."[31] I wrote this in the aftermath of leaving the cult I had been in. Many of the members were choosing to stay in the cult because they were receiving "good, secret, and hard-to-find information," yet they were selling out their character and virtue in order to acquire it. If you make knowledge or your own glorification your goal, you will sacrifice your

---

[31] https://www.alexlanshe.com/blog/my-personal-story-of-escaping-a-cult-part-2-the-brutal-truth-of-how-why-i-left

character and virtue whenever necessary to continue achieving those goals. Some members tried to justify themselves by saying that the good information would enable them to protect people better, so it wouldn't be prudent for them to leave the cult. Their underlying assumption was that a knowledgeable man can protect better than a virtuous one. I'm not so sure this is true. For though knowledge and skill are vitally important to protecting people, virtue forms the basis of your character, which determines your behavior. Mathematician and philosopher John Lennox is quoted as saying:

"2+2=4 but that never put 4 dollars in my pocket." — John Lennox[32]

In other words, knowledge doesn't necessarily lead to behavior (which produces outcomes). I think this is a vital distinction that many people today do not understand or fail to focus on. The solutions proposed to all your problems always seem to be more money, more possessions, more marriages, more government policies to help you, more protests, more education, more knowledge, more systems, and so on. Yet none of these things will solve any problem if the underlying virtues that inform your behavior are not addressed. Humility is truly where a protector starts and is

---

[32] https://en.wikipedia.org/wiki/John_Lennox

the foundation of all other virtues. It ensures the honesty necessary to make a brutal assessment of the reality of one's character, behavior, and life situation.

Myths of Humility

"Humility leads to strength and not to weakness. It is the highest form of self-respect to admit mistakes and to make amends for them." —John J. McCloy[33]

A myth that we must dispel right away is that humility is weakness. Nothing could be further from the truth. As a protector, if you are highly skilled and competent at fighting, it takes far greater nobility of spirit to not fight than it does to fight. Oftentimes it takes far greater self-control to exercise restraint than to take action. I would argue restraint is an action, and that one reason so many believe that humility is weakness is because they fail to accurately perceive that restraint and caution are actions! Making an active choice to restrain yourself is not passivity—it is the height of action! Don't get me wrong: There comes a time when you must physically fight to preserve life, and when that situation arises, you step up to the challenge and do your best. But how many fights could have been

---

[33] FBB, pg. 422

prevented if one or both parties had simply exercised a little humility?

The Problem of the Ego

Ego can get you into fights that never would have occurred if you had simply been humble. Road rage is a great example. How many people get shot, stabbed, or beaten with a baseball bat every year all across the world because they had to voice their anger to the other guy at being cut off on the highway? Humility neutralizes anger, and anger is a terrible enemy that will work against you in a fight. Anger clouds your judgment and can lead you to make costly mistakes. Humility is the underlying virtue of self-control and temperance (discussed in greater depth in Chapter 7, On Temperance). For now, suffice it to say that if you want to forge the virtue of self-control, you must begin to work on humility first.

More Ways to become Humble

What is another way you can become more humble? By actively reflecting back on a behavior and asking yourself: "What were my motivations in doing that?" If you find that your motivation was to be seen as a good person or because you enjoyed basking in your own limelight, then honestly admit that and resolve to do better next time. Many problems can be cured simply by having a resolute will.

Resolve today that you will examine your actions to discover what motivation lies at their heart. If you find that most of your actions are self-serving, you know that you have a great opportunity to begin again tomorrow with more humility and selflessness.

Humility and Reality

"Humility is to make a right estimate of oneself." — Charles Spurgeon[34]

Spurgeon's quote is spot on. Humility doesn't mean beating yourself into the dust, but making a correct view of yourself in the grand scheme of reality. The truth will prove to you that you are not as great as you might think, which is quite humbling. However, to beat yourself into the dust can be an indication of false humility. It actually takes greater humility to honestly admit your true place in the world instead of raising yourself higher or lower according to your own desires. Why? Because honestly admitting your true place requires you to die to your own desire to be either higher or lower. This is a monumental point I pray you take to heart because fostering this true humility will not only allow you to make the most accurate judgments in the real world, but will also give you tremendous peace.

---

[34] FBB, pg. 422

Humility is the Key to Adaptation and Preparation

Interviewee and 27-year veteran police officer Jack Colwell said:

"Humility allows you to adapt to your environment, which facilitates your survival."

Let that sink in for a moment. You know that on the battlefield of war and life, being able to cope and adapt to changing environments is crucial to staying alive and keeping others safe. But did you ever stop to think that humility is the underlying virtue that will more easily allow you to adapt? Think about it: When your environment changes (or your behavior), you must be honest enough to admit that. But if you lack humility, your pride will prevent this honesty from taking place. Humility precedes the required honesty to adapt to changing environments. What a brilliant insight from Jack. In order to adapt successfully to your environment, you must be prepared to adapt. Humility encourages you to be the perpetual student and the "Boy Scout" who is always prepared. Why? Because you admit that things could go wrong because you and life are not perfect. Bad things happen. Accidents happen. It is pride that says: "Nothing bad will happen to me today." Humility says: "I will prepare now for the day when things go wrong." We have discussed how, for protectors, preparation requires diligence and fortitude, but it also equally requires humility. Humility precedes the honesty necessary to admit that reality is dangerous and that preparation should be done in order to most effectively protect and preserve life.

What Are Your Limits?

Humility will also allow you to make an honest assessment of what your limitations are. This is vital to being a good protector. Overestimating your ability and/or skill could very easily lead to your death or that of a loved one. Underestimating your ability could lead to disastrous results as well. If you believe you are a good shot, but in reality rarely train with your firearm, humility will make you reflect and say: "You know, I've been shirking my firearm training. It's time to hit the range and find a good trainer for a home defense class." Humility will allow you to say: "You know, I'm good with a firearm, but if for some reason I cannot get to my gun or it doesn't work, I realize I don't have any unarmed or hand-to-hand skills. Maybe I should go find someone to teach me?"

Humility and Service

When I asked Interviewee Ward Smith to elaborate on what he meant by humility, he said: "Humility which leads to service." This gets right down to the pragmatic, protector level. Your humility should lead you to service. How will you serve others if you are not humble? If you have too much pride and believe that you should be served, how will you serve others? You won't. You cannot lie to yourself. Your spirit knows if you actually value serving others, or if you are only pretending. Strive to genuinely serve others by fostering the spirit of humility within yourself. How do you do this? Die to your own desires.

The Fruits of Humility

"The fruits of humility are love and peace." —Hebrew proverb[35]

How so? Because both extremes—that of excessive pride, and the extreme of beating yourself into dust—lead to an imbalance of soul and mind, which prevents you from being able to make a truthful and honest assessment of reality. Both extremes cloud your vision, can limit your awareness, and draw your focus not on the pursuit of truth, but on pursuing your own desires. Here is a practical example

---

[35] FBB, pg. 422

of what I am saying: Humility doesn't mean you always shrug off a compliment; it means dying to your own desires! If you constantly shrug off compliments (real compliments, not simply shady flattery) because you are "so humble," you actually move further away from true humility. Why? Because by constantly shrugging off the compliments, you are giving yourself what you want instead of humbly submitting to the will of another and taking the compliment.

How I Learned this Lesson

I was taught this powerful lesson in my life by a good friend, Bill Carrier. I met Bill and his wife Julie at a speaker's event in Los Angeles. As I got to know them better, Julie, who has a naturally joyful, bubbly, and grateful personality, was thanking me for something I did, and I brushed it off (because I'm "so humble" . . .). That is when Bill pulled me aside and said:

> **"Alex, you are denying Julie the ability to give you the gift she is trying to give you. I know you didn't think of it that way, but when you brush off the compliments that she sincerely wants to give you, you deny her an opportunity to be charitable."**

Wow. What a great lesson in true humility. I saw this among some of the interviewees. They were quick to cast off any compliments or recognition I gave them. I am not saying this comes from a place of bad intentions—far from it. I think most people who do this mean well (I know I did). But the reality is that it takes a greater act of humility to accept the compliment precisely because you don't want to. If I was truly considering Julie's feelings above my own, I would accept the compliment graciously, for that is what would build her up and give joy to her spirit. Ever since Bill taught me that lesson, I have practiced returning compliments with a good-natured "thank you" instead of "Who? Me? I'm a nobody, I don't deserve that."

How can you apply this discovery in your own life?

What praise, help, advice, or other gifts are you refusing on the grounds that you are "so humble"? Turn your thoughts to what would make the person giving you those things happy, and then act appropriately.

Why is Humility Important?

Why is this important to being a good protector? Because a true warrior and protector is interested in protecting people against violence. Maintaining good relationships and trying to make others happy neutralizes anger, hostility, contempt, and hatred. All of these could lead to violence acutely, or years down the road. A true protector has the broad-spectrum awareness that he or she has a duty to protect the hearts, minds, souls, and emotions of others, not simply to protect their bodies from physical threats. In many ways, protecting the body is the easiest way to protect someone. Being truly humble and taking a compliment with grace that you don't think you deserve can sometimes be more difficult. These are the small fires which turn into the infernos which light your character.

Humility as Your Personal Shield

True humility serves another great purpose in succeeding as a protector—it protects you from flattery and manipulation. There is no one on earth easier to control and manipulate than someone who has excessive pride and self-love. As a protector, you want to guard against this most vigorously. Your beacon and guide is truth, not flattery. How many people have been killed or injured because someone who was supposed to be a protector accepted a bribe, looked the other way when a partner did something wrong, filed some paperwork "incorrectly," or buried the truth? How many did these things in order to preserve human respect? A great many of them, I would wager. You protect yourself, and by extension others, from this type of corruption when you possess true humility.

Humility vs. Charm

Just as you accept a true compliment because it goes against your will, humility clears your vision so that you can more accurately perceive when someone is trying to manipulate to. Gavin de Becker writes a lot about how criminals attempt to manipulate people in his iconic book *The Gift of Fear*[36]. In one chapter, he discusses how charm is one tactic among many that criminals use to get what they want. Who is susceptible to the criminal's charming tactics? The one with the overinflated sense of self. Humble people can spot these types of charm tactics a mile away because they possess an honest view of themselves and do not spend too much time thinking about themselves. Men and women are equally susceptible to the charming tactics of others; it simply takes on different forms when it is done to one or the other. Guard against being manipulated and charmed by fostering the spirit of true humility. I am not saying that if you are victimized by a criminal's charm it means you lack humility. Oftentimes, people who are nurturers and who care for others make easy prey because they want to help so badly that they put themselves in vulnerable situations. It is a fact, however, that if

---

[36] https://www.amazon.com/Other-Survival-Signals-Protect-Violence/dp/0440508835/ref=sr_1_1?ie=UTF8&qid=1504627906&sr=8-1&keywords=the+gift+of+fear

you are puffed up with self-love and quite enjoy having your ego flattered and stroked, a criminal may be able to recognize that and use it to his or her advantage. Therefore, guard against flattery by immunizing yourself with humility.

Combine Humility with the Previous Virtues

If you pair humility with love, fortitude, and justice, you will become a formidable warrior. It is my belief that the virtuous warrior is the most able to successfully protect and preserve human life. Even someone who lacks the skills and knowledge of how to fight can still protect and be a warrior. Why? Because there is more to protection than just the physical fighting. What causes fights? What leads to conflict in the first place? A lack of virtue. Cowardly, selfish, immoral, and prideful human beings are far more likely to violate someone else's rights and to inflict violence and evil upon other human beings compared to those who are courageous, selfless, just, and humble. Don't you agree?

The Top Four Virtues

These first four chapters chronicle the four virtues that were the most referenced in my research conducted by interviewing 120 protectors. There are three more virtues that also were mentioned, which complement these first four quite well. One was already mentioned in this chapter. It is a virtue that is fast declining from our society, and one that a protector cannot go without. That virtue is the virtue of prudence.

In order to help you remember and utilize the seven virtues more effectively, I created seven corresponding postures for you to practice.

Why do I recommend you do this?

You and I remember and retain more information when we are physically moving. We are biomechanical creatures and assigning a physical posture to each virtue will help to anchor them in your mind. This posture was chosen because at first glance, it looks non-threatening and receptive – like humility. Like humility however, you are prepared, ready for action, and are in one of the primary protect positions where you are able to protect your face, head and vital organs. Strike this pose and say out loud, "I am humble." There will be a posture at the end of each chapter. If you want to play a game, try to guess why I chose each posture before reading the description. Let's see how accurate your intuition is. Each of the postures were chosen not merely for their aesthetic appearances but also due to the physical, martial, fighting applications they contain. Hidden within the seven postures are a myriad of fighting and combat applications that I show to my clients. If you want to discover what some of them are, subscribe to *The Anatomy of a Warrior Show*'s YouTube channel.

https://www.youtube.com/channel/UCB4Y_6Rwcgg1t6k2X-ZqDlg

Chapter 5: On Prudence

"Prudence is the necessary ingredient in all the virtues, without which they degenerate into folly and excess." — Jeremy Collier[37]

All the virtues you have heretofore acquired shall prove of little use to you if you lack this chapter's virtue: prudence. Prudence is the ability to discern and make appropriate judgments. This virtue is most essential to being a successful protector. What good is all your courage if you lack the ability to discern when to apply it? Prudence is also called common sense or good judgment. As a protector, you make a million tiny judgments throughout each day. If you are a parent, you know all too well how many tiny judgments you make every day to make sure your child is fed, clothed, and cared for. Knowing what decision and judgment to make, and why, is prudence. When to do what is another way of describing prudence.

Prudence and Action

Prudence does not mean that one is unable to take action—far from it. This is why prudence must be paired with fortitude, lest your prudence turn into timidity and passivity. The ability to accurately

[37] FBB, pg. 698

assess reality and come to conclusions and plans of action based on those conclusions is a vital skill for you to possess and forge. Notice, however, that merely discerning what reality is and making accurate judgments about it does not necessarily mean that you will take the appropriate actions related to these judgments. You can perceive and judge rightly and yet still behave incorrectly, or make a mistake in execution of your desired action, whether it is the right or wrong action. However, if you simply take loads of action with no prudence, you are likely to make a great many mistakes, which could cost you or your loved ones their lives. "Discretion is the better part of valor."

Common Sense

Interviewee and legendary protector Massad Ayoob talked about common sense. When you drill into the heart of common sense, what is it? I assert that it is the ability to make sound judgments based on sound observations and experience. Have you ever met someone who had a shrewd common sense about him or her? We've all met people like this: Someone who seems to know just what to do for any situation and event. These people may not be able to win on *Jeopardy* by regurgitating memorized facts, but they make good judgments. Similarly, do you know anyone you would say is a shrewd judge of human character, who just seems to be able to pinpoint what a person is about within seconds or minutes of meeting them? This is a person who has common sense. They are calling upon past experiences and observations to make predictions and judgments about things in the present and in the future. Developing this common sense is highly beneficial to you as a protector. Do you know anyone who you would say has a good BS detector? This could also be labeled under the heading of common sense. They just kind of know when someone is feeding them a line of crap. That is common sense, and it is based on the virtue of prudence.

How to Develop Prudence

How do you get better at making good judgments? Put yourself in uncomfortable situations that require you to stay alert and aware, and to act. Familiarity with a thing is the battleground of forging prudence. Unfortunately, there is no shortcut. You must get used to making judgments by making judgments. If this answer seems very simple, that's because it is. Virtue is very similar to the laws that govern exercise and building muscle. If you want bigger biceps, you must do exercises that work those muscles. Doing squats is a poor way to increase biceps size. Similarly with virtue, if you want to become more prudent, start making more intentional decisions and judgments. Pay attention to your environment, put down your cell phone, and start falling in love with human perception again.

More Ways to Develop Prudence

How else can you forge the virtue of prudence? When I interviewed Gavin de Becker, he talked about one thing in particular, which I believe will help you immensely: You have permission to become curious again. Let me say it again: You have permission to become curious again. Curiosity is what causes protectors to look at things and mull them over in their minds. Good protectors, Gavin says, can be curious about anything in their environments; even something as seemingly mundane as the paint on a wall. At the heart of curiosity is the love and ability to ask questions. To put this into practice, the next time you are stuck in a waiting room at the doctor's office, instead of just blankly sitting there or worse, vegging out on your cell phone, look around the room and deliberately focus on and be curious about the details. Ask questions about anything and everything. Avoid the urge to judge whether your questions are good or bad; at first, simply ask the questions. What colors can you see, what smells do you smell, and what sounds do you hear? What patterns can you recognize in the carpet, and why is it patterned that way? Notice the people around you. Try to think where someone could be hiding a weapon if they were nefarious. What objects in the room could be used as improvised weapons if need be? Where are the exits? The questions go on ad infinitum. The better you get at this game, the more details you can try to perceive. For example, instead of simply observing that the walls at your doctor's office are painted blue, dig deeper and ask: "What kind of blue, and is there a reason they chose this exact kind of blue?" This will help to bring clarity to your perception, which will in turn allow you to make judgments based on your perception. Visualize this process and game of asking very detailed questions about your environment as if you were sharpening a knife. The more detailed questions you can ask, the more you are sharpening your knife of curiosity. This is very important for you as a protector because being curious and asking questions is the first step toward becoming prudent. You cannot make accurate judgments if you cannot ask accurate questions. Apply this game to and ask questions about your environment, people, symbols within the environment, patterns you observe, behavior, and more. Get back in touch with your inner child and be curious again. The more familiarity and experience you gain doing this, the more you will notice human behavior that will inform your judgment for next time.

Human Behavior

If you want to become an even better protector, you should be a good student of human behavior and communication. You already have built-in biological and spiritual systems designed to make you a master at this. Intentionally focus on enhancing your knowledge of human behavior, and practice using your rational mind and subconscious mind to make judgments and discernments. This is why, when soldiers enter unknown territories, they seek to become familiar with as much as possible as soon as possible. Interviewee and former United States Marine Patrick Van Horne wrote about this in his fantastic book *Left of Bang*[38]. I highly recommend this read, as its discussion on combat profiling is precisely the sort of thing I am referring to. Gavin de Becker also touches on prudence (though he may not use that exact word) in his iconic work *The Gift of Fear*, where he talks about how your intuition is already designed to predict violent behavior.

---

[38] https://www.amazon.com/Left-Bang-Marine-Combat-Program-ebook/dp/B00L45NXF4/ref=sr_1_1?ie=UTF8&qid=1505865176&sr=8-1&keywords=left+of+bang

Intuition

One thing I will echo Gavin on is that you are predesigned to be a highly competent judge of human behavior. You possess a powerful tool, known as your intuition, which serves you well in making thousands of decisions each day, and operates largely outside the domain of your conscious thought. I share in Gavin's belief that you do not need an expert to teach you or to "unlock" your intuitive capabilities. You use intuition every day to make high-stakes predictions and to discern all matter of various phenomena. Similarly, I believe that all the virtues in this book are within your grasp and power to do and be right now, without the aid of experts and gurus.

My Personal Example of Prudence

In my personal life, it was my intuition which first told me that something was wrong with the cult leader I broke free from. Just a soft, quiet voice whispering to me to look into things further because something was wrong. I ignored my intuition for almost three years because I continued to rationalize away what my intuition was telling me—big mistake, and one that I will not be so likely to make again, thanks to learning the hard way. How did I know this? Because my intuition was making thousands of micro-judgments based on thousands of micro-observations. To perceive and judge wisely is the essence of prudence, and it oftentimes speaks through your little voice called the intuition. If you wish to be able to hear your intuitive voice even more clearly, you must practice listening to it. The more you ignore the soft whisper, the harder it becomes to hear. When you receive a gut feeling or reaction, at first, do not attempt to understand exactly what it is or where it came from. First, take it in and acknowledge its existence. Oftentimes, your subconscious knows something to be true even when your conscious mind does not. Practice active listening with your own subconscious mind as if you were listening to a dying man tell you where he buried $10,000,000. Think back into your past; did you ever do something that you knew in your gut you should not do? What were the results? Did you ever have a gut feeling telling you to do something, but you failed to do it? How did you feel later? This was your intuition speaking to you.

Prudence and Creativity

Prudence is an important virtue to pair with creativity. The more you can creatively attack a problem (or bad guy) the more freedom and choices you will discover, which could lead to various solutions. There is a reason "adapt and overcome" is an unofficial slogan of the Marine Corps. However, if you lack prudence, or the ability to judge, how are you supposed to adapt? If you cannot judge or perceive that tactic A is not working, how will you know to adapt to tactic B? Perhaps the best way to enhance your virtue of prudence is simply to spend time around people. Be an active student of human behavior—there is no better way to learn than by doing.

Rational Thought

Intuition is one element of prudence, but so is rational thought. Many judgments are made intuitively, and those very often when in the presence of true danger, but rational prudence is very important too. True prudence combines the power of your conscious and subconscious faculties, as both are very important and have their places in protecting. Being able to evaluate a crime scene coldly and rationally is critical for criminal investigators. A police officer's ability to accurately gather information about his community is invaluable. A soldier who did his homework and knows the local customs and terrain better than most is at a huge advantage, compared to those who lack this knowledge. In your life, if you can do a logical, stepwise analysis of: "If I do X, what are the potential outcomes?" you are using the virtue of prudence. Rational prudence is critical for the planning, preparation, and evaluation of violent events. Interviewee and former Russian Special Forces soldier Igor Livits spoke about how valuable it is for a protector to possess an analytical mind. What he is driving at is that you must be able to rationally evaluate and make good judgments based on your observations and perceptions. Analysis is mental, but it is informed by the virtue of prudence.

Wisdom

A prudent person is also said to be wise. Wisdom is basically the ability to perceive reality accurately and to conduct one's behavior appropriate to the circumstances. A wise man does the right thing, at the right time, in the right way. The first step is to be able to perceive and discern what that right thing to do is.

"To act coolly, intelligently, and prudently in perilous circumstances is the test of a man and also a nation." — Adlai Stevenson[39]

For you, as a protector, prudence becomes of the utmost importance because you may be in a situation where you have only seconds or milliseconds to perceive reality, make a decision, and then act upon it. Interviewee Rob "Waldo" Waldman is a retired Air Force fighter pilot who flew 65 combat missions. As a pilot, he had

---

[39] FBB, pg. 698

to make split-second decisions and then act upon them. One wrong judgment could have been fatal. That is just one example of a high-stakes situation in which prudence is of the utmost importance.

High-Stakes Decisions

Are you married? If so, would you say that choosing a spouse was a high-stakes decision? I am not married yet, but I know that choosing a life partner requires the utmost prudence. Your life and future happiness are quite literally at stake if you choose poorly—not to mention the life and happiness of your spouse and any potential children you produce. It is therefore very important to make these decisions with a cool, rational head and not in the heat of passion— as romantic as that is portrayed to be in Hollywood. Just as prudence will help you when choosing a spouse, it will be hugely helpful when you decide who to let babysit your children, whom you invest money with for a business deal, where you go to school, and so on. You make countless judgments like these each day. Pay attention to them now, and be intentional about what judgments you make, especially over highly consequential decisions, and why you make them. Always ask yourself: "Why did I decide to do X?" "How did I come to that conclusion?"

Prudence and Preparation

Prudence is a virtue that helps you to prepare for the worst. Sound judgment dictates that your plans could go wrong, so you need to be prepared and have some contingency plans. When this is your job, for example in executive protection, you should exhaust all options you can possibly think of to be sure you stay one step (and preferably more) ahead of would-be assassins or stalkers. This same approach applies to you as a parent, business owner, spouse, employee, or other protector. Suppose you get a flat tire while driving home on a dark, rainy night. You go out to change your tire, only to realize your cell phone is dead and you have no flashlight. Prudence will dictate that once you survive this encounter, your next trip will be to Wal-Mart to get a $20 flashlight whose permanent home will be inside your vehicle. Prudence will cause you to prepare for such an event so that if it should happen again, you are ready. Ideally, you can learn from the prudence of other protectors and warriors (as you are right now by reading this book) so that you do not have to experience everything yourself.

What is the Point of Prudence?

For you, as a protector, the bottom line is this: The more prudence you possess, the better you are able to accurately and effectively identify threats. Prudence calculates risk and reward, and it identifies threats of all natures. Interviewee, mother, and competition shooter Julie Golob said that a protector

". . . Must be able to identify threats."

This is the bottom line with prudence. Your job as a protector is to identify threats and neutralize them—or prevent them from ever occurring. You cannot do this without the virtue of prudence.

The Liz Lazarus Story

Let me tell you a story about interviewee and survivor of a home invasion and attempted rape, Liz Lazarus. Unbeknownst to Liz, she had been stalked by someone who was intent on raping her. Liz had never experienced anything like this before, and what was about to happen would transform her life forever. Liz had a flimsy latch on her bedroom door that she typically did not lock. But the night of the home invasion, something whispered to her that she should lock it. In her own words, locking that door was:

". . . only enough to stop him [the would-be rapist] from sneaking up on me. He still broke down the door, but my latching the door saved me because it gave me enough time to wake up and realize what was going on. I didn't

have to wake up with the knife at my throat." —Liz

Lazarus

Liz may be alive today due to trusting her instincts and judgment to lock her bedroom door. What is the moral of the story for you? Trust your instinct. Do not question its validity when it is trying to keep you safe. Your instinct may be wrong about some things, but it always has your self-preservation at heart. If you want to delve deeper into Liz's story, she wrote about it in her first book, *Free of Malice*[40], a fictional thriller using her real-life encounter as the impetus and catalyst for the story.

Interconnectivity of Virtue

Remember that all virtue is interconnected; so much so, that it has been said that if you attain perfection of any one virtue you necessarily attain perfection in all of them. I challenge you to ponder the interconnectivity, for example, between prudence and humility. What exactly is their relationship to one another? What about love and fortitude? Examine all the possible different combinations long enough, and you will see how they all complement and enhance and are connected to each other like Borromean rings—remove one ring and the whole structure falls apart. What is love without

---

[40] http://www.lizlazarus.com/

fortitude? What is prudence without justice? What is courage without temperance? What is justice without love? They all form a cohesive, dynamic singularity, and all feed off of and give life to each other.

Consequences

If you make a judgment that proves to be incorrect or that causes you to suffer some type of ill consequences, this is the type of judgment you should most analyze. Why did things go wrong? Was it something you failed to perceive, or was it something totally outside your control? How could you have been better prepared to see things more clearly? This is a very important exercise to engage in.

My Personal Story with Prudence

When I left the cult, I learned a valuable lesson relating to prudence. I learned that allowing human respect to cloud your judgment leads to detrimental outcomes. Can you think of a time when you were blinded by having too much respect for what other people thought about you? Peer pressure is very real for you, me, and all protectors. We all have people we love and respect, but prudence dictates that we should not allow such things to cloud our ability to perceive the truth and reality. As a protector, you are called to make the higher sacrifice of walking the path of truth, so that you can always be in a position to combat evil so that others don't have to. In truth, it is in your best interest to walk the path of truth for yourself as well. I believe that there is no greater way to feel peace and happiness than to align yourself with the truth. Aligning yourself with the truth is the greatest way I know to ensure that you make proper judgments and see what there is to see.

The Enemies of Prudence

Prudence is also highly important for you to develop because you will more accurately be able to perceive your own limitations and weaknesses. Prudence dictates that you should occasionally examine yourself for weaknesses in training, diet, health, how well you are taking care of your relationships, your mental health, spiritual health, and so on. Prudence, paired with honesty, will give you better judgment. Be careful to avoid self-deception. If you are not honest with yourself, your discernment will become flawed, and your vision will become more and more opaque, like looking through foggy window. Excessive pride will also cloud prudence, as will anger and anxiety. Use fortitude to combat anxiety (there is no better cure for anxiety than work) and humility to neutralize anger and pride. Pride leads to a lack of honesty and excessive self-love, which clouds your judgment. Anger also shuts down your rational mind, which can be very deleterious when you are trying to decide upon a course of action. Anxiety mentally removes you from the present and has you focusing excessively on either the past or the future. Prudence dictates that you appropriately weigh and measure the value of past, present, and future, rather than becoming hyper-focused on any one of them.

Another Major Enemy

Another major enemy of prudence is despair. Despair clouds the judgment immensely. According to the American Foundation for Suicide Prevention, nearly 45,000 Americans commit suicide each year, placing it as the 10th leading cause of death in the United States[41]. Prudence would dictate that it isn't wise to murder yourself, but prudence can be eclipsed by despair. As a protector, you must protect yourself from yourself as well as from external threats. U.S. soldiers swear an oath to defend the Constitution from enemies both foreign and domestic, and it is the same for you and me. Foreign is the bad guy who breaks into your house. Domestic is your family and yourself.

---

[41] https://afsp.org/about-suicide/suicide-statistics/

The Antidote for Despair

What is the antidote for despair? This is a heavy question, and it is a touchy subject for many who have known someone who took their own life. I believe that there is a ready antidote that can be obtained by anyone who wants it, provided they put forth the effort—as is the case for the pursuit of any virtue. All good things require effort, and our next virtue is no different. Virtue number 6, and perhaps the best antidote to despair that mankind has ever discovered, is the virtue of faith.

In order to help you remember and utilize the seven virtues more effectively, I created seven corresponding postures for you to practice.

Why do I recommend you do this?

You and I remember and retain far more information when we are physically moving. We are biomechanical creatures and assigning a physical posture to each virtue will help to anchor them in your mind. This posture was chosen because at the heart of the virtue of prudence lies discernment. This is the "thinking-man" posture which should cause you to remember to be prudent and make wise judgments as a result of your thinking and perception. Strike this pose and say out loud, "I am prudent!" There will be a posture at the end of each chapter. If you want to play a game, try to guess why I chose each posture before reading the description. Let's see how accurate your intuition is. Each of the postures were chosen not merely for their aesthetic appearances but also due to the physical, martial, fighting applications they contain. Hidden within the seven postures are a myriad of fighting and combat applications that I show to my clients. If you want to discover what some of them are, subscribe to *The Anatomy of a Warrior Show*'s YouTube channel.

https://www.youtube.com/channel/UCB4Y_6Rwcgg1t6k2X-ZqDlg

Chapter 6: On Faith

"Faith is kept alive in us, and gathers strength more from practice than from speculations." —Joseph Addison[42]

To my knowledge, scientists, philosophers, and theologians alike have found no greater remedy for despair than the virtue of faith. Many of the interviewees talked about the necessity for a protector to believe in a power higher than themselves.

Faith in God

Several interviewees were quite open about their belief in God, and that this belief gives them strength to carry on and to do the job of a protector. All interviewees I spoke with who specifically mentioned God admitted to being Christian. I am a traditional Roman Catholic, and I believe that God plays a vital role in my journey as a protector and in being able to continue fighting the good fight and to avoid despair. Let's face it, as a protector, especially a professional, you may see some horrible things. You may even see things that defy description, and you may struggle to fathom how there can be so much evil in the world. Many people, when faced with this reality,

---

[42] FBB, pg. 272

cannot cope if they rely only on the strength within themselves. It is a tremendous blessing to have an infinite God you can lay these troubles before and to have an all-merciful, all-just God you can serve. As we have discussed, to be a protector is to be in service to others. Some of the interviewees simply take that principle one step higher and strive to serve the Great General of the universe: God. I strive to do my best, and it gives me great hope and strength. As often as I can, I mentally and spiritually prepare for each day to be my last—as it well could be. Faith in God and the afterlife helps me to prevent feelings of despair and nihilism.

Nihilism

From one protector to another, my friend, I ask you, would you say that our experiment with nihilism and postmodernism has been helpful or destructive to our societies? Has trying to pretend that we are a sophisticated society, too grown up for such silly things as faith, been helpful in preserving lives and ending suffering? I do not believe so. It is hard to imagine anyone arguing that believing in nihilism could motivate you to live the sacrificial life of a protector. Nihilism comes from the Latin *nihil*, and English *-ism*, literally translating to "nothing-ism." If your ultimate faith resides in "nothing-ism," will you sacrifice your life for the protection of others? Will you live a life of sacrifice, denying yourself the many pleasures you want for the sake of others? Perhaps you would, but many would not.

Where is Your Faith?

It is worth noting that even if all you have faith in is nihilism itself, you still have faith in something. If you have faith only in yourself and your own capabilities, you still have faith in something. If you have faith in your teammates and in your training, you have faith in something. If you have faith in philosophy, religion, observational science, your five senses, your intellect, or something else, you still have faith in something. What do you believe? Where do you place your faith? It is worth noting that you can have faith in yourself and faith in God. You can have faith in many different things. Most of them are not mutually exclusive. If you have faith in multiple things, it simply becomes a question of which is the deepest, and which is your ultimate source? Where does the buck finally stop? This is a hierarchy for most people. I challenge you to explore your hierarchy of faith. What is on it, and what is the sequence or ranking of things on it? How you discover this is by digging deeper into your beliefs by asking questions. Ask yourself, "Where is my faith?" and when you have an answer, ask yourself further, "Where does my faith in that come from?" Keep playing this game until you reach the bottom to discover the ultimate source of your faith. The great thing about what you place your faith in is that it's entirely your choice. You can change it whenever you want. If what you have been placing your faith in isn't doing it for you anymore, seek something greater. You have permission to seek and change where you place your faith.

The Capt. Charlie Plumb Story

Capt. Plumb was not shy in telling me that his faith in God played a crucial role in helping him not only to survive his Vietnam internment, but to forgive his enemies, to love, and to hope. He believed God had a purpose in his being imprisoned, and that if he had faith, God would see him through.

> **"And we know that all things work together for good to them that love God, to them who are the called according to his purpose." —Romans 8:28**[43]

In a truly remarkable moment of candor and honesty, Capt. Plumb told me in our interview, after quoting this Bible verse, that he had to examine whether he really believed this verse was true. Wow. He decided to try to prove the truth of this verse during his internment in Vietnam. Regardless whether you are a Christian or not, this man's faith cannot be underestimated as a vital factor in making him a

---

[43]
https://www.biblegateway.com/passage/?search=Romans+8%3A28&version=KJV

successful protector. His faith allowed him to keep his spirits and his wits about him to ensure not only his survival, but the survival of many comrades imprisoned with him. I extol you not to focus on where Capt. Plumb places his faith, but on the vital importance his faith had in keeping him and others alive.

Sheepdogs and the Great Shepherd

Lt. Col. Dave Grossman was another man who declared that faith plays a vital role in giving the protector strength and hope to carry on despite all adversity. In another remarkable moment of honesty, the Colonel said to me:

> **"I really believe that it is hard to be a good sheepdog without knowing the Good Shepherd."**

I share in his sentiment.

Faith in a Higher Purpose

"Faith is the great motive power, and no man realizes his full possibilities unless he has the deep conviction that life is eternally important and that his work well done is part of an unending plan." —President Calvin Coolidge[44]

---

[44] FBB, pg. 272

Many of the interviewees also spoke about having faith that all things happen for a reason and that your sacrifices mean something in the grand scheme of things. In short, they believe there is a higher purpose to things. It is not necessary to believe in God, strictly speaking, to believe that life has a higher purpose. The bottom line is: Do you believe in something that transcends you, or not? Some of the interviewees mentioned having this transcendent belief without paying reference to any particular religion or deity. Do you believe your life has meaning and purpose? Why or why not?

Faith in Yourself

"Faith that the thing can be done is essential to any great achievement." —Thomas Carruthers[45]

If you are facing a deadly encounter with another human being, an animal, or even a natural disaster, an unwavering faith that you will survive to see another day is paramount to successfully surviving that encounter. Program yourself now that you will survive by never speaking one ill word of your survival capabilities. Be defiant and say to yourself: "I will not die this way." If you die despite this attitude, you will have done all you can to survive. If you lack this attitude and conviction and faith, it may cause you to give up or quit

---

[45] FBB, pg. 273

before you should have. Defiantly resist and have faith that you will survive.

The Jared Reston Story

Interviewee and police officer Jared Reston has an incredible story. While off duty, he and a partner were asked to help a local mall's security department with some shoplifters. He never would have suspected that making an arrest on a shoplifter would turn into a deadly force encounter. While the first suspect was apprehended, the second took off running. Officer Reston ended up chasing the suspect down and getting into a physical fighting match with the suspect, who would not comply with commands to cease resisting even after Reston had identified himself as an officer. While they were fighting, Officer Reston was shot in the face at point-blank range, which damaged his teeth and jaw and exited his neck. He was hit with seven rounds from a .45 caliber handgun. Reston would later cite his belief in himself and his defiance that: "I will not let this son of a bitch kill me like this," as driving motivations that carried him through to win the day. Reston, despite having been shot multiple times, returned fire on the suspect. The suspect began charging toward Reston in an effort to get closer, presumably to be better able to deal the death shot. Reston, however, was putting good rounds into his target, and the suspect crumpled over as he reached Reston. While the suspect was still alive, Reston placed three rounds into the suspect's head at close range, ending the fight and neutralizing the threat. He was awarded the Presidential Medal of Valor. His story is a harrowing but moving account of the will to live[46]. He had faith that he was going to survive, and he refused to die in that moment. He later would say, when interviewed by fellow interviewee Dave "Buck Savage" Smith on PoliceOne.com, that when he thought about his wife and one-year-old child, it motivated him to say: "I will not die like this. Not today." Obviously, in addition to faith, Officer Reston needed to possess the skills and to take the necessary actions he took to save his life. But would he have taken those actions if he did not have faith that he could? Thankfully, he did survive, so we will never know the answer to that question.

Questions about Faith

Officer Reston's case brings up a crucial question: Does action precede faith, or does faith precede action? Is faith itself an action? Does it change depending on the circumstance? These are very deep questions that I confess I cannot answer. What I do believe is that you can actively believe something by making a conscious, free

---

[46] https://www.policeone.com/police-heroes/videos/5955882-Will-to-Win-Jared-Reston/

will choice. I also believe that you and I possess many beliefs that we have not examined closely in our conscious minds. Perhaps we should examine them more frequently. Just as a computer will scan for viruses and malware and then do a cleanup, you should do the same with your mind and heart. What detrimental beliefs (viruses) have crept into your mind, heart, and soul without you knowing?

Faith in Others

When I interviewed J. Mason, a Navy SEAL and founding cadre member of SEAL Team 6, he spoke about the missions that SEALS engage in and how each team member is utterly committed to every member of the team and to the mission. This faith in each other, paired with a common goal (the mission), is what allows SEAL teams to be so successful. They would do anything for a teammate, and that utter surrender of their own self-interests is what fosters trust. I interviewed current or former members of other Special Forces groups, such as Green Berets, Army Rangers, as well as Marines, and they all spoke of a similar faith in their teammates that J. Mason spoke of regarding the Navy SEALS. Whom can you trust? Whom do you have faith in? As a protector, you know that you cannot do it all—no matter how tempting it is to be like Batman and go solo. In fact, a good protector admits his or her limitations and gets a team of people they trust assembled to achieve the same goal. If you are married, you and your spouse should be unified in your mission to keep each other safe from all violence and conflict. If you have children, you should be united on that goal as well. I believe that if you push all your loved ones away, you begin the process of isolation that could lead to your very demise. Have enough faith in others to train them and give them a task in protecting you and others. Remember, they have the instinct to protect you, just as you have the instinct to protect them. Lions in a pride will pick off the Cape buffalo that is sick and alone, not the strong and surrounded.

Crazy Buffalo Story

Speaking of buffalo, interviewee Michael Dorn told me about a crazy experience he had with a bunch of African trackers when they suddenly discovered they were surrounded by Cape buffaloes[47]. If you have never seen one, follow the link in the footnote to see how massive they are. It will help you to appreciate the story even more. Michael Dorn, his team, and the African trackers were armed, but against a charging Cape buffalo their guns would be nearly useless if the bullets did not find the heart or the brain. Dorn and his team

---

[47] http://www.nationalgeographic.com/animals/mammals/w/water-buffalo/

waited intensely for several minutes to see what the buffalo would do. Fortunately, calm and patience proved to be all that was necessary that day to survive, as the buffalo ended up moving on without incident. Make no mistake, however, Dorn and his team were in mortal danger while surrounded by these large animals. If one of them had felt threatened and made a charge at Dorn or his men, things could have been disastrous.

Why do I tell you this story?

Because Michael spoke of the profound trust the trackers have among each other. This trust is founded upon a faith in one another and in each other's abilities. For Michael Dorn, seeing how they handled themselves in the bush was a powerful discovery about just how important faith and trust in your teammates are. This trust is based on their highly developed skills and capabilities, which are honed due to necessity. If you fail at your job as an African tracker, you get eaten, gored, or run over by a large animal. Necessity is the mother of invention.

How does this relate to you?

If you have a family, be like the African trackers and train them. Get them involved as much as possible in your protection plans—both against human violence and natural disasters. Faith is enhanced and heightened by works. If African trackers can develop such powerful trust, it is possible for you and me to do so as well. Who is on your team?

Faith and Works

"In the same way, faith by itself, if it is not accompanied by action, is dead." —James 2:17[48]

This, I think, is one reason why you may have scoffed when you read in the previous chapter that we were going to be talking about faith in this chapter. Somewhere along the line, "faith" became something you just blindly believe, grounded in nothing more than a mere emotional whim. This is not the type of faith the interviewees and I are referring to. The faith I am speaking of is accompanied by action. You are a protector, a man or woman of action. Action and faith are not mutually exclusive. Rather, they are mutually *in*clusive. You exercise faith every day when you wake up from sleeping and go to set your feet on the floor. You have faith, based on past experience and action, that your feet will not be magnetically repelled from the floor, rendering you incapable of standing. You trust (have faith) that your feet will strike the floor as usual. You do not begin to imagine that when the sun rises tomorrow, its face will

---

[48] https://www.biblegateway.com/passage/?search=James+2%3A17

be colored a deep, navy blue. Past experience tells you otherwise. You have faith that when you shoot your firearm, the bullet will proceed in the direction you fired it and not in some other random direction. The interviewees and I are not asking you, as a protector, to have blind faith. It is not blind faith that makes you believe the sun's face will not be blue tomorrow. Past experience informs your faith. You've never seen a navy blue sun, and the rational law of cause and effect would demand that such a thing has a reason for not happening. Likewise, as a protector, you do not have blind faith that you will survive the violence that faces you. Past experience proves you are a survivor! Do you see how faith is accompanied by works? I believe that a good protector has belief and pairs it with action. Action without guidance by true and right beliefs will lead to random and dangerous consequences. Faith without works will produce no fruit, and in a pragmatic sense will mean that you are actually protecting nobody. Faith plus works is the winning formula. If you lack faith in you or your teammate's abilities to protect, seek out proper training. Get fit, get healthy, and find some personal protection trainers to help you get the skills you require to be a good protector. Action increases faith, and faith can lead to action. If you have trained well and prepared, there is no reason to be overly worried. Trust that the work you have done has prepared you to succeed and survive. You may have a lack of faith in yourself if you know you have failed to prepare adequately. Preparation is the antidote to anxiety and lack of faith. If you are not confident in your own abilities, this is simply a signal to train; go practice and go study so that you can be ready for violence if it ever visits you.

False Dichotomies

By faith, I don't mean to say that you should become naive to the dangers of the world. Far from it. Faith is rational, calming, and peace-filling. Faith is what gives you hope that after a horrible day, a new sun will rise. Faith and reason go together; they are not adversaries, as you may have heard or been taught. It isn't "faith vs. reason," but rather "What is the proper combination and hierarchy of faith and reason?"

It isn't "faith vs. science," either. Somebody lied to you. The men and women I interviewed are some of the finest technicians and scientists of their craft in the world. Yet many of them cited faith as being a very important virtue to succeed as a protector. It is possible to have faith and to be pragmatic, to be realistic and hopeful. I believe that a protector strives for the ability to do that which is appropriate in any circumstance to protect human beings from violence, evil, and suffering. Do not buy into these false dichotomies that the world offers you. They are lies and they limit your ability be a successful protector.

Faith in New Beginnings

Another element of faith that I suggest you examine is whether or not you have the faith and belief that people can make amends and turn over a new leaf. I firmly believe that any person who humbles themselves, abandons past wrongs, and takes up the mantle of striving for virtue can turn their life around. I believe that if you do not believe in new beginnings, it makes sacrificing for others much more difficult. Why would you sacrifice for someone if you truly thought there was no way they could benefit or change by seeing your good example? Do you really have faith that your actions can make someone else and the world better?

> **"There are many persons that smile on hearing talk of building a better world and say that the world cares nothing for that. These persons have lost faith in people and God because of their own mistakes." —John S. Bonnell, D.D.[49]**

---

[49] FBB, pg. 272

This doesn't mean you expect that anyone who sees your sacrifice will change his or her life for the better. Some people will never change, because they choose not to. But I believe that if you believe it is at least possible for someone to change for the better, you will be more successful at being a protector who serves.

Speak Faith

"The power of life and death is in the tongue." — Proverbs 18:21[50]

One way you can be assured that you increase the virtue of faith, is to speak more faith into your life. This is not New Age nonsense, but battle-tested wisdom coming to you from 120 professional protectors. As it says in Proverbs, you have the power of life in your tongue. Words you speak can elicit ideas and thoughts, which serve to heal, inspire, and protect, or they can tear down, destroy, and create despair. If you can become even better at controlling the words that come out of your mouth, you can become an even better protector. The words you speak or don't speak have an effect on your degree of faith and on what you place your faith in. Each and

---

[50]

https://www.biblegateway.com/passage/?search=Proverbs+18%3A21&version=KJV

every word you speak has the power to give or take life. Speak wisely and with prudence.

The Final Analysis

Ultimately, you must place your faith somewhere in something. Your mind is simply too small and finite to know everything with certainty. Therefore, faith is required. There is one final virtue that is required for you to be a successful protector. In a way, it is the glue that holds everything else together. Like prudence, it is an old-fashioned word that carries with it depth and richness of meaning. Our final virtue is called temperance.

In order to help you remember and utilize the seven virtues more effectively, I created seven corresponding postures for you to practice.

Why do I recommend you do this?

You and I remember and retain more information when we are physically moving. We are biomechanical creatures and assigning a physical posture to each virtue will help to anchor them in your mind. This posture was chosen because kneeling on one leg is the classic pose of prayer, offering and submission. You can fold the hands in whatever way suits you. Strike this pose and say out loud, "I have faith in ___!" (Fill in the blank with who or what you place your ultimate faith in). There will be a posture at the end of each chapter. If you want to play a game, try to guess why I chose each posture before reading the description. Let's see how accurate your intuition is. Each of the postures were chosen not merely for their aesthetic appearances but also due to the physical, martial, fighting applications they contain. Hidden within the seven postures are a myriad of fighting and combat applications that I show to my clients. If you want to discover what some of them are, subscribe to *The Anatomy of a Warrior Show*'s YouTube channel.

https://www.youtube.com/channel/UCB4Y_6Rwcgg1t6k2X-ZqDlg

Chapter 7: On Temperance

"Fortify yourself with moderation; for this is an

impregnable fortress." —Epictetus[51]

If you are going to be successful as a protector, you should strive to be temperate in your indulgences. Temperance is sometimes referred to as "moderation." Temperance is also sometimes defined as self-control. We will explore all these various meanings and how they relate to you becoming an even better protector.

Self-Control

Being able to control your emotions, your stress response, and your actions is vital to protecting others. Have you ever been so mad at someone you said or did something you shouldn't have? Welcome to the club. The problem is, if you do this to strangers (or even to people you know) you may send them over the edge, and they could lash out with violence, violence that could have been totally prevented if you had exercised temperance. Temperance can be thought of as self-restraint, the ability to be in control of your decisions, emotions, and even your desires. Sometimes you may desire something that you shouldn't want, but if you are striving for

---

[51] FBB, pg. 581

temperance you will immediately seek to control even your thoughts as quickly as possible. Why do I believe you should do this? Because I believe that thoughts lead to feelings, which lead to actions. Therefore, seeking to control and restrain your mind is vital in your development as a protector. How does this relate to a physical fight or confrontation? Let me give you an example. Being able to hold back and wait for the appropriate moment to strike can mean the difference between life and death. John Correia, interviewee and founder of the Active Self Protection (ASP) YouTube channel[52], talks a great deal about waiting for your turn in a fight. This is borne out by the many hundreds of dash cam and security camera footage videos his channel shows. Inevitably, an assailant will surprise someone or a group of people and have the upper hand. But oftentimes, if one of the victims is patient and waits for an opening (i.e., stays in control and doesn't panic) the criminal will present one. I can recall a half dozen videos on John's channel illustrating the virtue of temperance and its importance in a fight. I highly recommend you check out John's channel in the link and watch some videos to get a real-world look into what these violent situations look like.

---

[52] https://www.youtube.com/channel/UCsE_m2z1NrvF2ImeNWh84mw

Temperance vs. Inaction

Being temperate doesn't mean that you fail to act—quite the contrary. Temperance is controlling when and how you act. A protector with a great deal of temperance is capable of unleashing some of the fastest and most effective violence known to man and can bring themselves out of that state when the threat has been neutralized. Temperance is precisely the virtue that gives you the ability to do what is necessary in any situation. If that means you must be a shoulder for a victim to cry on, you can do it. If that means you must be the one to end the life of a violent aggressor to save innocent lives, you can do that as well. Prudence discerns what reality is and informs you of what action to take, and temperance controls that action so that you do what you wish to do to get the response you desire. No more, no less.

The Antidote to Overkill

Temperance is the antidote to overkill. Temperance will give you the ability to do just enough and no more, no less. When we have seen instances of police brutality or civilian overkill, what virtue is never being demonstrated? Temperance. The individuals in these instances have lost control, which leads to their use of excessive violence. A truly temperate warrior is able to be fiercely patient. Self-control is also the beginning of wisdom, which helps you to make more effective and prudent decisions.

Temperance as Balance

In fighting, temperance can be likened to balance. Temperance is what allows you to maintain balance and control your stability. Think of temperance as a stance or base. Just like a fighting base, there are bases that provide more mobility, others that provide more stability, and still others that are combinations of the two. Temperance is your base, which affords you stability and mobility of character.

Moderation

"Everything that exceeds the bounds of moderation has an unstable foundation." —Seneca[53]

Temperance has also been referred to as "moderation." While I don't like simply classifying it in this way because "moderation" is not a verb or action, temperance should often lead you to a place of moderation. Always taking rash action without thinking or seeking counsel can lead to disastrous consequences, but so can thinking too much and failing to act. "Discretion is the better part of valor," they say, but sometimes people place too much value on being a

---

[53] FBB, pg. 581

planner or a doer. Be what the situation needs you to be and have the self-control to do it. For our purposes here, it is better to understand "moderation" as "enough." Too little or too much is immoderate. This means that if a situation calls for extreme violence, you do it because that is what the situation calls for. To not enact that violence to protect others when the situation demands it is actually to be immoderate, to not do or give enough to neutralize the threat. Moderation, therefore, is simply enough. Enough to neutralize the threat.

The Lesson of the Columbine Massacre

Do not confuse Temperance with hesitation. Temperance is a virtue, hesitation is not. Caution does not necessarily equal temperance either; though temperance does often call for one to be cautious. Let me give you an example of where caution was given too high a value at the cost of life. One of the interviewees was a man who was a SWAT member responding to the Columbine Massacre. He told me that more people died that day than needed to die due to their hesitation to enter the building. They were on the scene and ready to go, but they were told to wait. Some said this was because they were trying to gather all the facts before they took action to avoid making a costly mistake. This may very well have been the intention, but when people are in the process of being shot, you don't exactly have a lot of time. The interviewee regrets not going in sooner and knows in his heart that they could have saved lives if they hadn't waited so long and hesitated. Do not confuse temperance with this hesitation or overly cautiousness. Temperance is merely the self-control to execute the decisions made by prudence. If anything, the failure of SWAT to enter the building was an error in judgment (prudence), not self-control. They used self-control to wait because they were told to wait by the higher-ups who made a judgment call (prudence).

Regaining Control after a Fight

Temperance also means you can regain calmness after a bout of violent action. This should be your goal. Temperance after a fight exists on several different levels:

- Your thoughts: As a protector, you should seek to temper your thoughts. Uncontrolled and undisciplined thoughts can lead to uncontrollable behavior. If you cannot control your thoughts in calm, quiet moments, how will you control yourself in the chaos of a home invasion?

- Your emotions: Anger, fear, and similar emotions can do great damage to you in and after a fight if you are unable to control them. They cloud your judgment and can cause you to overcommit to a technique or application. Use the virtue of temperance to control your emotions as best as possible.

- Your body: If you allow the body's heart rate to get close to or above 200 beats per minute, you will have a very hard time remaining in control of your actions, as panic starts to set in. Read Lt. Col. Dave Grossman's classic work *On Combat*[54] for a more detailed analysis of what happens to the body during and after a bout with violence.

Feedback Loop

The human being is an incredible feedback loop that can go in both directions. What do I mean? I mean that actions, physical motions, and exercise can change your mental and emotional state, while simultaneously, your mental and emotional state can change your physical state. Your will can change your body, and your body can change your will. It is the goal of acquiring the virtue of temperance to make your body evermore the servant of your will and intellect, rather than the other way around. The body is fickle, sensitive to pain and stimulation, and often wants to quit well before the mind

---

[54] https://www.amazon.com/Combat-Psychology-Physiology-Deadly-Conflict/dp/0964920549/ref=sr_1_1?ie=UTF8&qid=1505499526&sr=8-1&keywords=On+Combat

and soul do. The intellect can operate on principles and logical truths that are not subject to change, but they will take you only as far as the body can be disciplined to follow.

How to Become More Temperate

How do you become more temperate? Intentionally deny yourself little things that you want. If you want a second bowl of ice cream, tell yourself no and then do not eat any more ice cream. Just like a muscle that has not been moved for a long time, your temperance muscle may be weak from ill use. It can grow quite strong rather quickly, however, when you achieve these small victories of the will. If you tell yourself "you should go for a walk," go for the walk. It is not so much to achieve the health benefits of walking (although that is clearly a good thing, too) but to build up your temperance muscle again. In this day of instant gratification, cell phones, and Google searches, we are accustomed to quick fixes. Temperance is not like this, however. You must do the "exercise" necessary to build this temperance muscle up again.

My Personal Story of Temperance

In my personal life, after leaving the cult, I had to consciously exercise the virtue of temperance with regard to handling people's responses to how and why I left. Some people responded with concern, others with anger. It took a great deal of self-control to either ignore or respond civilly to those who were sending me angry emails. It also required a great deal of self-control to accept someone's decision to remain in the cult despite my having just told them the truth about the leader and the group. I say all this not to impress you, but to impress upon you the importance of self-control and temperance in your life. What situations have you gone through that required self-control? How well did you meet that challenge? Do you have room for improvement? So do I. Opportunity abounds in the quest to become more temperate.

Letting Go

Another element of temperance is letting go of things you cannot control. I had to learn this the hard way when I left the cult. Friends I had hoped would leave the cult with me did not leave, and that frustrated me. How could they not see the clear truth and get out? I cannot control them, and temperance understands that you can only control yourself. Temperance was an important virtue for me to utilize during my cult experience, as I was also feeling emotions of sadness, anger, and regret. Temperance allowed me to feel those things but also to prevent those emotions from controlling me. As a result, I do not have bitterness towards the cult leader or other members. I easily could have gone down that route had I not been focusing on being temperate and controlling my feelings and responses to this difficult situation.

What Has a Lack of Temperance Cost You?

Imagine a time when you overreacted. What did it cost you? Did you hurt someone or just yourself? What price would you pay to be able to go back and do it over, but with temperance instead of letting your emotions get the best of you? Understand, this is no easy task and there is no end to this quest of pursuing temperance, or any of the virtues in this book. It is a lifelong struggle. I do not have all this figured out and perfectly acted upon in my life. Far from it. The truth is, you will never achieve perfection of the virtues, but you can get farther up the ladder. The infinite well of virtue means there is no limit to how much you can grow your character. You can become more and more virtuous for your entire life, and that is an encouraging thought.

Temperance for Longevity

"Power exercised with violence has seldom been of long duration, but temper and moderation generally produce permanence in all things." —Seneca[55]

---

[55] FBB, pg. 581

Do you want lasting personal peace and the ability to be a calm, protective refuge for your loved ones? Start building yourself a foundation out of the virtue of temperance. When you indulge, be in control of what and when you indulge. Make a decision and keep to it. This is the true essence of temperance. If you decide you will eat two bowls of ice cream, eat them with joy and then be done. Do not stress over every little decision you make and say: "Am I being temperate enough or too temperate?" Make your decision and then keep to it, even in seemingly inconsequential things like whether or not you stay awake for another half hour instead of going to bed. If you said you would go to bed after your TV show and it ends, then go to bed. This practice gives your will control over your body and will build tremendous self-confidence.

Michael Fletcher's Story of Calm

I asked interviewee and former 82nd Airborne Army Ranger Michael Fletcher what his greatest moment as a protector was. I was expecting him to talk about when he attempted to rescue fellow soldiers from burning while he was on fire after a plane crashed and exploded nearby. But he didn't say that. Instead, he told me a story of when he was a paramedic and he delivered twins in the back of the ambulance. He saw that as his greatest moment. He told me that bringing new life into the world is about as good a job as a protector can do—delivering twins during the Christmas season in the back of an ambulance as a paramedic. Wow. This is a man who truly understands the essence of what it means to be a warrior and a protector.

Why do I tell you this story?

Because Michael had spoken to me earlier in our interview about the importance of calmness to a protector. Calmness is a byproduct of self-control. You cannot be calm if you are not in control of yourself. He said it took calm for him to be able to deliver those twins. It obviously was not part of the plan to have to deliver them in the ambulance—ideally, the mother would have made it to the hospital. But those babies were coming whether he or the mother liked it or not. He remained calm and simply took the necessary actions that were within his control to take to ensure the safest delivery possible for those newborn babies and the mother. This, my friend, is what it means to be a warrior. Never let anyone tell you different.

The Myth of Self-Confidence

I see so many people selling confidence: speakers, authors, coaches, entrepreneurs, groups, associations, and more. "Be confident this" and "be confident that." "You're perfect just the way you are" and "love yourself!" As if these silly mantras can create true self-confidence within a person. Do you want to know where true confidence comes from? From the ability to control yourself. Self-control brings you faith and hope, at least in yourself if nothing else. Self-control leads to the discipline to develop real skills, another source of confidence. Self-control and skills. It is my belief that the rest of the rah-rah stuff people try to sell to you is vacuous and empty. It offers you a false promise of quick confidence in a can. All you have to do is heat it up in the microwave! If only this were true. Confidence cannot be faked, and it doesn't come from rah-rah speeches. It comes from doing what you say you're going to do (using integrity and self-control) and developing real skills. If you want to become a more confident protector, start practicing self-control and get busy training. The more temperance you acquire and the more skills you possess, the more confidently you will protect others.

Final Thoughts on the Seven Virtues

Temperance is the virtue which controls all the others. A crucial membrane that wraps up the organ of virtue. Courage or fortitude gives you the power to act; love serves as the source from which you draw your motivation and inspiration to act; justice serves as the boundaries, the parameters of what is right and wrong, good and evil; humility serves as the foundation of perceiving reality as it is because it holds your ego in check, it serves as the foundation to preventing excess or depletion; prudence gives you the ability to discern and make accurate judgements about reality; faith is what provides you with a higher vision, mission and purpose that will stabilize you in an unstable world; temperance gives you the ability to always deliver just the right dose of whatever solution is required to neutralize a threat. These seven virtues, if you cultivate them, will serve to help you better prepare for, protect against, and prevent interpersonal violence. The more individuals that take up this task, the greater the effect we will see in society. Will you commit to living like a warrior? Will you dedicate yourself to honing these virtues in your own life? It is my sincere desire and hope that you will.

In order to help you remember and utilize the seven virtues more effectively, I created seven corresponding postures for you to practice.

Why do I recommend you do this?

You and I remember and retain more information when we are physically moving. We are biomechanical creatures and assigning a physical posture to each virtue will help to anchor them in your mind. This posture was chosen because the low hand position communicates the notion of restraint and "no." A large part of temperance is the self-control to restrain your emotions and to be able to deny yourself. Strike this pose and say out loud, "I am temperate!" There will be a posture at the end of each chapter. If you want to play a game, try to guess why I chose each posture before reading the description. Let's see how accurate your intuition is. Each of the postures were chosen not merely for their aesthetic appearances but also due to the physical, martial, fighting applications they contain. Hidden within the seven postures are a myriad of fighting and combat applications that I show to my clients. If you want to discover what some of them are, subscribe to *The*

Anatomy of a Warrior Show's YouTube channel.

https://www.youtube.com/channel/UCB4Y_6Rwcgg1t6k2X-ZqDlg

Postscript: A Call to Action

What is my vision for you? I believe that you are a warrior who boldly has the courage and fortitude to persist through any adversity and challenge; you love with a selfless and sacrificial love, you are compelled forward by an unwavering sense of justice, morality, and a need to do the right thing; you have impeccable character forged by honoring your word and your commitments. You prudently discern what appropriate actions to take; you live in utter service to others because your humility reminds you that without others you are nothing; and you operate fully in control of yourself by exercising temperance over your life. If you are not this person yet, I believe you can be. Is it hard to reach that point? Of course it is. But do you know what is harder? Not being virtuous. Reread the last paragraph, but substitute all the virtues with their opposites. What would that look like?

"You are an entitled victim who cowardly avoids doing any work to better yourself or others, you shrink from every form of adversity, and waste your life away watching television because you lack the courage to risk failure. You selfishly strive to consume as much as possible and take from anyone and everyone you meet. You give nothing to them in return, and are confused when people leave you; how could they not wish to dote on you constantly? You have a completely relativistic sense of justice and are pretty much okay with any behavior as long as it gets you what you want. You are not sure if morality even exists, and you don't really care to know. You do not keep your word, and as such you have no friends because no one can trust you. You make bad decision after bad decision because you fail to care enough to prudently discern what choices you should make. You are so consumed with self-love that there is not a drop of humility in your body. This causes you to be an insufferable know-it-all who has achieved nothing, who no one can stand to be around. Finally, lacking all manner of self-control, your body is in shambles, your mind is cluttered, and your soul a festering mess of illicit desires and thoughts. You long ago gave up the desire to better yourself, and in this state you continue to worsen, if that were possible, until you die."

Does that sound appealing? That is the opposite life that many people lead each day because they choose not to strive for virtue.

You cannot afford to live this way. Virtue must be your pursuit because you have chosen to take up the mantle of a protector. Other people's lives are at stake, and they need you. You can physically survive for a time in the vice-ridden state, but what kind of life is that? How sad, when you have every capacity to live otherwise, that you should choose such a state. I know you won't choose that state, but many do. They perceive the path of virtue to be too difficult, so they do not try. Let me ask you something. Isn't anything difficult the first time you try it? What happened to you the first time you tried to read, or ride a bike, or ask a girl out on a date? You probably failed miserably, and it was probably quite hard! But what happened after you practiced those things? They not only got easier, but you began to enjoy them. The same is true for the warrior virtues, my friend. If this task seems too monumental, begin with a single step:

> **"The journey of a thousand miles begins with a single step." —Lao Tzu[56]**

What is the very first virtue you can strive to improve upon? What action is the very first action you can take toward pursuing that virtue? Think about this, and then go do it! Do you know what the

---

[56] https://www.brainyquote.com/quotes/quotes/l/laotzu137141.html

hardest part of writing this book was? Sitting down to type up the first words of the first chapter. After that, it was relatively smooth sailing. But overcoming the inertia of not writing to change over to a state of writing was quite challenging. What helped me to move past this inertia was reminding myself of the consequences of my inaction. How many people were not reading this book yet because I was taking too much time to get it published? How many lives was I failing to positively impact because I wasn't getting started? How much money for myself and the charities I've partnered with for this book was lost because I wasn't getting started? If the warrior's journey of virtue ever seems too difficult, remind yourself of what is at stake and what the consequences of your inaction are. Think of the other people who need you, but you won't be able to help them because you didn't care enough to forge a virtuous character for yourself. I recently returned from a business event in Los Angeles, California. I had the great pleasure of hearing world famous speaker, Les Brown, speak. He said something while speaking that I felt was directed to me and me alone. He said: "How many of you are speakers?" A large percentage of the crowd raised their hands. Les said: "That's good, because the world needs you now more than ever before." I was struck by his words. "The world needs you now more than ever before." I realized that every day I failed to write, speak, and get my message of the warrior virtues to you was a day I was wasting. People need to read this book; they need to implement the pursuit of these virtues into their lives, especially you, as a protector. I realized that these warrior virtues transcended all walks of life, all businesses, all relationships, and all occupations or life callings. They are at the very core of what it means to live well and to be a good human being. I submit Les Brown's words to you: "The world needs you now more than ever before." He wasn't just talking to me, he was talking to you and anyone who is a protector and a warrior. The world needs our warriors now more than ever before: principled, virtuous warriors who will do what is right in the face of pure evil, and who live to serve their fellow man. "The world needs you now more than ever before." This is your time. People are counting on you. I am counting on you, your nation is counting on you, and the world is counting on you.

"The only thing necessary for evil to prevail is for good men to do nothing." —Edmund Burke[57]

You are a warrior. You take action. You are not a nihilist. The warrior's journey and pursuit of virtue is the real self-help journey.

---

[57] https://www.brainyquote.com/quotes/quotes/e/edmundburk377528.html

Unlike all the motivational speeches that fade as soon as they end, the pursuit of virtue is endless. It gives purpose to each and every action, thought, emotion, joy, suffering, and problem you face. How? Because any action you take, any thought you think, and any emotion you have can all be viewed through the prism of forging virtue or weakening virtue. You can do this, my friend. Begin to control yourself today in something small. Simply telling yourself to go do one push-up and then doing it begins the journey of taking control of your life with temperance. Wash, rinse, repeat until that is easy, and then move on to greater challenges. Pretty soon, you'll be a fully realized warrior of virtue making a great impact on the lives of your family, friends, nation, the world, and yourself.

"The world needs you now more than ever before."—

Les Brown

Live with virtue, my friend!

Alex Lanshe

Afterword – Gavin de Becker

Bestselling Author, <u>The Gift of Fear</u>

Protection is a high calling, one that has existed throughout human history, one that allows at-risk people to conduct the work they are here for, and live the lives they are here to live. Protection can be seen as a burden, bother or an intrusion, but at the moment of an attack, it is always highly valued. In my study of thousands of attacks on protected persons, many important things were learned, but none more important than this:

> *The overwhelming majority of public figure attacks are over in less than five seconds.* Within just those few seconds, all the damage that will be done has been done.

That five-second statistic could be discouraging, because it grants very little time for protectors to respond effectively. However, embedded within that five-second statistic is an encouraging lesson: Attackers are even more handicapped by the speeding clock than are protectors, and when protectors are in a position and mindset to respond, they will prevail; almost always. Being in position is physics, but having the mindset to prevail – that's a different matter – and a matter on which this book might help. I've learned that the most valuable mindset for protection derives from a strong sense of mission, which derives from an element that Alex has explored in these pages: Virtue.

- Virtue inspires you and others to do their best
- Virtue reminds you of why you chose to protect others

Another key element of protection is confidence, which derives from readiness and learning. What would inspire someone to train for hours, days, weeks and years for an event that is almost certainly never to happen? Virtue.

What might students of protection learn from training that they didn't know at the start? They'd learn that public figure attackers who fired handguns at targets within 25-feet usually hit their targets, while attackers who fired handguns from farther away than 25-feet almost never hit their targets. This means that safety is nearly assured when the physical set-up provides 25 feet or more between the protected person and the nearest members of the general public. 25-feet emerges as a magic number, but you have to first know that number in order to gain the magic. Effective protectors spend a lot of time preparing for every public appearance, and much of their energy is applied to influencing space – negotiating for more space between the stage and the seats, more space between the red carpet and stanchions, in short, more space between the protected person and those who might try to attempt harm. Protectors might learn that attacks in the US are most likely to be undertaken by lone assailants (87% of the time). Or that attacks outside the US are most likely committed by multiple assailants (71%). They might earn that firearms are the most common weapons of attack (71%), or that bombs succeed at killing intended targets only slightly more often than they fail (57% of the time). They might learn that 64% of attacks happen when the protected person is in or around the car, and these attacks succeed an astonishing 77% of the time. While this kind information has value for developing protective strategies, once an attack has commenced, almost all knowledge becomes useless mental clutter. Perhaps the single most valuable thing a protector could know is _when_ future attacks will happen — and that we do know, precisely:

One hundred percent of all attacks happen

at exactly the same time: Now.

The only time _anything_ can happen is in the present moment. Everything else is a memory (the past) or a fantasy (the future), and nothing in the past or future can hurt your protectee. An attacker's moment of commitment is always in the Now, and if you hope to meet him there, you too must be in the Now. You could place yourself in the perfect position for foiling an attack (many bodyguards have), and yet if you are not present in the moment, *pre-sent* as it were, your body being there is not likely to be of any value. Some (not most) protectors work to maintain physical readiness, which is admirable. Still, it's the mind that must first be properly prepared, the mind that controls the hands, arms, eyes, and ears. Just as a computer functions best when loaded with accurate and relevant data, any committed protector must summon up virtue and learn all about protection.

You reading this book and every other book you can find on the topic is the expression of your virtue. I don't know you, but I already know and respect your commitment to learn. Keep reading, keep learning, keep teaching, and always work toward mastery. Virtue will get you there.

Gavin de Becker

The Interviewee List

120 interviews were conducted over a 2.5 year period gathering the research for this book. Please browse this list to see the caliber of individuals that were interviewed and do not hesitate to reach out to those who have contact information listed.

Name & Contact Info	Bio
Adam Turk tdog241@comcast.net	Lieutenant, Greeley Police Department, Colorado
Alexis Artwohl, PhD www.alexisartwohl.com	Author of *Deadly Force Encounters*; PhD Psychologist; National Speaker
Amanda Collins collins.amanda85@gmail.com	Founding Director of T.E.A.R.S Speak (Teaching & Empowering Assault/ Rape Survivors); Rape Survivor and Public Speaker
Bernie Sahadi	Former US Marine; Graduate in Business from MIT; Special Forces Trainer

Betsy Brantner Smith sgtbetsysmith@gmail.com	29 year veteran of Illinois law enforcement (now retired), police trainer, author and expert, owner of The Winning Mind LLC at www.femaleforces.com.
Bill Jeans http://panteao.com/instructors/bill-jeans/	Former US Marine & Vietnam War Veteran; 21 years as CA police officer (Ret.); hired as Operations manager at Gunsite by Col. Jeff Cooper (7 years in that role – Ret.)
Brian Condron MD bpcondron@comcast.net	Addiction psychiatrist Student of Systema
Cameron Hager	Ret. Police and SWAT Officer
Carrie Lightfoot www.thewellarmedwoman.com www.twawshootingchapters.org 888-572-7730 Carrie@thewellarmedwoman.com	Owner - The Well-Armed Woman, LLC Founder/Chairman of the Board - The Well-Armed Woman Shooting Chapters Co-host, "The Women's Gun Show" Podcast

Charles "Sid" Heal H9692@healbuilders.com	Author of *Sound Doctrine* and *Field Command*, President of California Association of Tactical Officers.
Charles "Chip" Huth Charles.huth@kcpd.org	26 years of law enforcement experience; Commander of Kansas City, MO Police Department's Special Operations Division; Has planned and coordinated and executed over 2500 high-risk tactical operations; Licensed national defensive tactics trainer; court-certified expert; State of MO defensive tactics subject matter expert; Senior consultant for the Arbinger Institute; Lives in Kansas City with his wife Shelly.
Capt. Charlie Plumb www.CharliePlumb.com Charlie@CharliePlumb.com	Naval Academy graduate, Top Gun Fighter Pilot and 6 Year POW in Vietnam; International Speaker on *LEADERSHIP UNDER PRESSURE* and Author of *I'm No Hero.*

Christopher Dockter	US Marine Corps Infantry US Marshals Service
Anonymous	Special Missions Operator from Ft. Bragg
Chuck Taylor www.chucktaylorasaa.com	Director, American Small Arms Academy since 1980. Former US Army Officer with extensive combat experience, credited with developing many of the tactical and shooting techniques used today by both military and police agencies. Also a well-known firearms writer and consultant with more than 1000 published articles and four successful books on weapons and tactics. Has also trained the individual bodyguards and armed security officers for several high-profile political and corporate figures and the general armed forces and Spec. Ops units of several nations.

Clint Smith www.thunderranchinc.com info@thunderranchinc.com	Combat decorated Vietnam veteran with two Infantry/C.A.P. tours U.S. Marine Corps 1967-1970. Police officer for seven years serving as Firearms Instructor and SWAT DM. Served as Operations Officer and Senior Instructor American Pistol Institute /Gunsite.1980-1983. Started International Training Consultants, Inc. From 1983 -1993. Director of Training for Heckler & Koch 1986 President of Thunder Ranch Inc. now is in 25th year 1993-2018. Published over 500 articles in American Handgunner, GUNS, American Cop, and SWAT magazines. Credited for the Urban Rifle concepts used by many today. Wrote the book on Urban Rifle and started Thunder Ranch Online Training. Clint continues today to teach every class with his wife Heidi at Thunder Ranch in the mountains near Lakeview Oregon

Craig Allen	Police and SWAT Officer; former US Marine
Curtis Cook	SWAT Team Leader and responder to the Virginia Tech Massacre; Former US Navy; Tactical SCUBA Rescuer (Ret.)
Dan Cahill	Deputy Chief, Anaheim Police Department, CA
Lt. Col. Dave Grossman www.Killology.com http://sheepdogknifeandgun.com/	Author of Pulitzer Prize Nominated book, *On Killing* and *On Combat;* Former US Army Ranger; featured on FOX News and many other media outlets
Dave Smith Email: thebucksavage@gmail.com Website: www.jdbucksavage.com Facebook fan page as "JD Buck Savage."	Internationally known speaker, writer and law enforcement expert. He began his police career in Arizona and in 1980 he developed the popular "JD Buck Savage" video training series. He was the lead instructor for the Calibre Press "Street Survival" seminar from 1983 to 1985, and was instrumental in

	developing Calibre's timeless "<u>Tactical Edge</u>" officer survival book. In 1989, he joined the Law Enforcement Television Network (LETN), developing and hosting cutting-edge police, security and public safety training as its Director of Education and was the general manager of Calibre Press until January of 2002. Continued to instruct the "Street Survival" seminar through 2012. Interviewed hundreds of police officers involved in deadly force situations and authored hundreds of related articles. Continues to train internationally and is the host of the award-winning PoliceOne.com "Roll Call Reality Training" segments. Author of the popular book *In My Sights*
Dave Spaulding <u>www.handguncombatives.com</u>	Lieutenant, Montgomery County (OH) S.O. Retired

Dave Young www.armatraining.com www.vistelar.com www.yourfamilydefense.com www.usfightingsystems.com	Director and Founder Arma Training, US Fighting Systems and Your Family Defense and Co-Founder of Vistelar
David Scott Man	Green Beret Lt. Col. (Ret.); Author of *Game Changers*; founder of Stability Group
Dick Caster, Ed.D rjcaster@gmail.com	Past Executive Director, National Association of School Resource Officers. Instructor, Tactical Defense Institute, Ohio Attorney General School Safety Task Force.
Donald Goodman dgoodman188@gmail.com	Chief of Police, Radford, Virginia. Former Operations Captain, Blacksburg Virginia Police Department
Donn Kraemer dbkraemer@prodigy.net	Retired Lakewood CO PD (35+ yrs.), Columbine HS rescuer, past-Pres. Rocky Mountain Tactical Team Assn., former CPT US Army Engineers, BS Engineering

Donna Angevine donna.angevine@gmail.com	Victor of violent home invasion; private self-defense, personal safety, and defensive handgun instructor
Erick Brown ebrown1481@gmail.com	Sergeant, Prince George's County Police Department (MD) Retired.
Frank Shankwitz www.wishman1.com	Air Force Veteran; The Creator and A Founder of the Make-A-Wish Foundation; 42 year law enforcement career-Motorcycle Officer Arizona Highway Patrol, Narcotics and Homicide Detective - Arizona Department of Public Safety.
Gary Klugiewicz gklugiewicz@vistelar.com 414-688-5572 www.vistelar.com	Gary T. Klugiewicz is a retired captain from the Milwaukee County Sheriff's Office. He currently the director of training for the Vistelar's Verbal Defense & Influence training program. He is internationally known for his performance-based conflict management and defensive tactics training programs.

Gary Shaw ghshaw57@gmail.com	27 years with the Texas Department of Public Safety; Highway Patrol, Narcotics, Texas Rangers.
Gavin de Becker https://gavindebecker.com/	Gavin de Becker is widely regarded as a leading expert in public figure protection. He is the bestselling author of *The Gift of Fear*, and *JUST 2 SECONDS*.
George T. Williams gtwilliams@cuttingedgetraining.org www.cuttingedgetraining.org 360.410.0804	Director of Training for Cutting Edge Training, LLC. He has been a police training specialist nationally and internationally for three and half decades. Since 1991, he's been expert witness in federal and state courts on police force, tactics, and procedures. Develops and provides unique, revolutionary, and sometimes evolutionary training integrating force skills, weapons, tactical principle and law and policy to achieve reasonable conduct. He's the author to two books and had over 300 articles published.

Georges Rahbani georges@rahbaniinc.com	Personal Protection Trainer; long-time student of Massad Ayoob
Colonel Gilbert S Palmer Jr (Deceased) & Stephen M Palmer gsp660431@reagan.com	Col. Palmer flew reconnaissance missions in the Vietnam War and was shot down and killed in service. His son, Stephen Palmer, served as a character witness for Col. Palmer
Gordon Graham http://www.gordongraham.com/about.html	33 year CA Law Enforcement veteran; Juris Doctorate; Risk Management Consultant
Grant Cunningham www.grantcunningham.com	Grant Cunningham is an author, teacher, and consultant in the areas of self-defense, personal safety, home and family defense, preparedness, and instructor development. He is the author of many popular books on those subjects and teaches workshops across the U.S.

Greg Allen	El Paso, TX Chief of Police
Greg Ferency gferency@itota.us	Narcotics detective currently assigned to a Federal Task Force.
Greg Williams	Former US Army & LEO; Expert in predictive analysis
Gregory Stevens gbs1704@gmail.com	Officer Stevens is a 39 Year active veteran Police Officer from the Garland Police Department in Garland, Texas. He was the 104th recipient of the Law Enforcement Congressional Medal of Valor, presented to him by President Barack Obama in 2016, at a ceremony conducted in the East Room of the White House.

Howard Gambrill Clark, Ph.D. clark@aya.yale.edu	Yale graduate, Dr. Clark has 20 years of experience in counterterrorism: Marines (Iraq, Afghanistan, and Philippines), White House, Homeland Security, Special Operations Command, and author of numerous books.
Igor Livits igor@aresprotectioninc.com	Executive Director Ares Protection, Inc.; Former SF
Jack Colwell unleashingrespect@gmail.com	Jack is the Director of The Arbinger Institute's Public Safety Practice. He retired from the Kansas City, MO Police Department. He is the coauthor of the book *Unleashing the Power of Unconditional Respect: Transforming Law Enforcement and Police Training*-CRC Press (June 2010).

Jack Hoban jhoban@rgi.co	Jack is a co-founder and Subject Matter Expert for the US Marine Corps Martial Arts Program (MCMAP), President of Resolution Group International (RGI), and author of *The Ethical Warrior*.
Jackson Short	Former SWAT Team member and current police commander.
James Hamilton james.hamilton@gavindebecker.com	Vice President of Protection Strategies for Gavin de Becker and Associates. 23 years of law enforcement experience, FBI and local Sheriff's Office.
Jamie Buffalari buffalari@icloud.com	Executive Protection and Corporate Security veteran
Jared Reston http://www.restongrouptraining.com/bios.aspx	LEO for Jacksonville PD (SWAT); Awarded Presidential Medal of Valor

Jason Czupryn Lt Jason Czupryn Terre Haute Police Department 1211 Wabash Av Terre Haute, IN 47807 Jason.Czupryn@TerreHaute.IN.gov 812-244-2226	Lieutenant - SWAT Team Commander Terre Haute Police Department (Indiana). 17 years and still going… Split between patrol and investigations and SWAT. 15 years on SWAT as Entry, Assistant Team Leader, Team Leader, Assistant Commander and current Commander.
Jeff Hall http://www.forceoptions.net/about.php	35 year martial arts and law enforcement career; featured on the History Channel's, *Sniper: Deadliest Missions* for winning an air to ground firefight
Jeff Rhodes rhodesjeff@aol.com (828) 687-1571	Owner and Director of Center for Martial Arts USA. Rhodes has been training in Judo, Ju Jutsu and Karate for 40 years. Contracted employee at the North Carolina Justice Academy.
Jeff Trotter	28 year Police veteran; Former US Army

Jermaine Galloway https://www.tallcopsaysstop.com/	Law Enforcement Drug Specialist; Youth speaker against drugs
Joe Autera jautera@vehicledynamics.net	Former NCO in the US Army, 25 years of private sector experience planning, managing and participating in executive protection, secure transportation and surveillance detection operations in moderate and high risk locales across the globe. Currently President & CEO of Tony Scotti's Vehicle Dynamics Institute, one of the world's foremost providers of evasive driving training to private sector security, government, military, and law enforcement professionals.
Joe Keil operationrush@hotmail.com	27 Year Career with Manitowoc Sheriff Department, 17 year as a K9 Handler, Author of *When Just Say No Doesn't Work* and *Operation RUSH a guide to criminal patrol*

John "Andy" Anderson SF SGM (R) 14855 W. 54th Ave Golden Co. 80403 303-279-9203	25 years in US Army Special Forces (Green Berets), retiring at the rank of Sergeant Major. During that time, completed all special forces and special operations training, was a demolitions expert and instructor, an instructor at the Special Forces John F. Kennedy Special Warfare School, hand to hand combat instructor, military freefall instructor, and taught weapons and tactics. Served two tours in Vietnam working with such elite units as CCN (Command and Control North) and the Mike Force (Mobile Strike Force) as part of MACV/SOG.
John Benner https://tdiohio.com/staff/	Military MP in Vietnam War; Police Officer from 1971-Present; Runs TDI Ohio doing Force on Force and Defensive Training; has armed over 100 school administrations

John Correia www.activeselfprotection.com www.youtube.com/activeselfprotection john@activeselfprotection.com	Founder and owner, Active Self Protection; former US Navy
John Giduck john@circon.org	Homeland Security professor and author.
John Hanuska jhanuska@wmtwp.com	Patrol Sergeant West Manchester Township Police Department Tactical Commander York County, PA Quick Response Team
J. Mason	(Ret.) Special Forces
John Patterson elwoodman@aol.com	Law enforcement officer for 37 years (patrol officer to chief of police). U.S. Army officer for 8 years - Vietnam Veteran - company commander and military advisor. Decorated for valor & achievement.

Jose Rodriguez	(Ret.) US Marine; Served as US Embassy Guard as Marine; 20 year Police and SWAT veteran
Julie Golob www.juliegolob.com	US Army veteran; world champion, instructor and author of SHOOT: Your Guide to Shooting Competition
Keith Cunningham www.milcun.com	Partner at MilCun Training Center, co-author of *The Wind Book for Rifle Shooters* and *Secrets of Mental Marksmanship.*
Ken Murray murray.ken@RBTA.net	Author of *Training at the Speed of Life - The Definitive Textbook for Police and Military Reality Based Training*, Founder of the Reality Based Training Association, Co-Founder, SIMUNITION

Kevin Benson Kbenson355@hotmail.com	Colonel, US Army retired. Commanded a US Army tank battalion, 3-8 Cavalry. Served as the lead planner for the 2003 invasion of Iraq and assisted in the planning for the withdrawal from Iraq in 2010/11.
Kevin Burke Kevindre2014@gmail.com	Deputy Sheriff, Racine County Sheriff's Office, WI
Kevin Dillon (Lt. - Ret) kfd@policecombat.com www.policecombat.com www.diffusionstrategies.com	25 Years law enforcement, Founder of L.O.C.K.U.P. ® Police Combat Systems, Internationally recognized speaker and trainer.
Kimberly Corban www.KimberlyCorban.com	Rape Survivor, Public Speaker & Sexual Assault Advocate

Larry Lindenman www.pointdriventraining.com www.ciprotect.com	Point Driven Training, Illinois State Police Lieutenant (ret.), ISP SWAT - Squad Leader Instructor, Director Lake County Metropolitan Enforcement Group, Clark International - Regional Manager of Operations, Range at 355 Training; Coordinator, Carlson Gracie Team, Brazilian Jiu Jutsu black belt.
Linda Miller www.milcun.com	Partner at MilCun Training Center, co-author of *The Wind Book for Rifle Shooters* and *Secrets of Mental Marksmanship.*
Liz Lazarus www.lizlazarus.com liz@lizlazarus.com	Home Invasion Survivor & 2A advocate, Author of psychological, legal thrillers: *Free of Malice* and *Plea for Justice*
Marty Hayes, J.D. www.firearmsacademy.com	Director and Founder, The Firearms Academy of Seattle, President and Founder of Armed Citizens' Legal Defense Network, Inc. 20+ years as police officer, 30+ years as firearms trainer.

Massad Ayoob http://massadayoobgroup.com	43-year cop, 38-year expert witness in shooting cases, author of multiple books on weapons and self-defense.
Anonymous	Undercover Agent
Matt Sekela matt@tacticalsynergy.ca	30 year cop, 20 years SWAT, Global Operations Manager International Tactical Officers Training Association. Owner Tactical Synergy
Michael Dorn www.safehavensinternational.org	Executive Director Safe Havens International Co-author *Staying Alive - How to Act Fast and Survive Deadly Encounters*
Michael Dunphy, PhD mdunphy@walsh.edu	45 year veteran of classical and modern martial training. Expert in close-quarter combative tactics. 40 years as a professional in higher education; Ph.D. in Biochemistry and Dean of the School of Arts and Sciences at Walsh University

Michael Fletcher michaelfletcher1911@gmail.com	Safety and Security Director for K-12 public school district. SWAT operator, paramedic, and former soldier in the 82nd Airborne.
Anonymous	US Special Forces
Michael Gillitzer michael.gillitzer@semperfifund.org	Master Sergeant USMC.
Mike Herr MichaelHerr017@gmail.com	Celebrity/Artist Personal Security; 15 years in Systema
Mike Conner	Maryland Law enforcement officer with over 20 years' experience, Criminal Interdiction Expert
Mildred "Missy" O'Linn Senior Partner, Manning, Kass, Ellrod, Ramirez, Trester Email: mko@manningllp.com	Juris Doctorate from the University of Akron School of Law in Akron, Ohio; Police officer for eight years at the Kent State University Police Department; Legal and Technical Advisor for the Law Enforcement Television Network, Inc. (LETN); Los Angeles County Deputy Sheriff's Association's recipient

	of the Award for Civilian Leadership; Meritorious Service Award from the City of Gretna, Louisiana Police Department for her assistance to law enforcement in the aftermath of Hurricane Katrina; Recipient of the California P.O.S.T. Lifetime Achievement Award for Excellence in Law Enforcement Training.
Patrick Van Horne www.cp-journal.com	Co-author of *Left of Bang: How the Marine Corps' Combat Hunter Program Can Save Your Life.* Co-Founder of The CP Journal. Served as a Marine Corps infantry officer for seven years.
Paul Watson	12 year LEO in SC; Former Air Force Reserve deployed North of Baghdad - received Army Ranger coin for his role in supporting them; Runs Martial training center in SC for youth and adults

Captain Pete Bethune pete.bethune@gmail.com	Captain at Earthrace Conservation, Producer of "The Operatives" TV Show, Published Author, Wildlife Ranger, Holder of World Record for circling the globe by powerboat.
Peter Soulis pd.soulis@gmail.com	Thirty year law enforcement veteran. Founder of Soulis Shooting Systems LLC, Internationally recognized speaker and trainer.
Phil Chalmers https://philchalmers.com/	Author of *Inside the Mind of a Teen Killer*, and *True Lies*; Police Trainer
Philip Kurman PKurmanPhD@gmail.com	Psychologist, lecturer, and educator. Competitive shooter. Experienced US Army Ranger, university educator and former Eagle Scout.

Randy Sutton http://randylsutton.com/bio/	Author; 25+ rear Police Career (NJ and Las Vegas); 4 Deadly Force Encounters Survived, National Spokesman for Blue Lives Matter; One of the most decorated Las Vegas Officers of all time.
Randy Watt randy@srwsplops.com	Police Chief, Ogden, Utah; Colonel (ret.) U.S. Army Special Forces. President/Founder, SRW Strategic and Tactical Special Operations Training and Services, Inc.
Richard Fike fikeadvisor@gmail.com www.cqcsi.com	U.S. Army Special Operations Officer (ret.) Director, Close Quarter Combat Skills Institute providing unique skill sets to "At Risk" individuals and organizations. Motivational Speaker.
Richard Sacco	Former US Navy; Capt. Canton Ohio Fire Department (33 years of service); Black belt in Martial Science

RK Miller	28 year LEO and 17 year SWAT Officer, US Marine Vietnam War Vet
Lt. Col. Rob "Waldo" Waldman Waldo@YourWingman.com **www.YourWingman.com**	Hall of Fame leadership speaker, executive coach, and author of the *New York Times* and *Wall Street Journal* bestseller **Never Fly Solo**. A combat decorated fighter pilot, he is an expert in helping leaders and organizations accelerate performance in changing environments.
Rob Erikson	United States Marine Veteran
Rob Pincus http://www.icetraining.us/robpincus.html	Author; Firearms Trainer to Military, Police and Private Citizens; Founder of I.C.E. Training Company
Roberto DiGiulio	12 year Police Officer; Former SWAT officer

Ron Camacho rcamacho1505@gmail.com	Police Chief of the Chambersburg Police Department and International Police Trainer
Ronald McCarthy http://www.lapdauthors.com/ronald_mc carthy.html	Legendary LAPD SWAT Officer; Active in SLA Shootout; Former US Navy
Ronald Lousberg ronsteelfoot@hotmail.com	World Sabaki Challenge Full Contact Karate Champion / 38 years Martial Arts training
Rory Miller www.chirontraining.com	Author of *Meditations on Violence*; *Facing Violence* and others. Former corrections officer.
Scott Schwarzer	Radford, VA SWAT Leader
Steve Bentz steve_b_17404@yahoo.com Facebook: Russian Martial Arts of Lancaster	Head instructor at Russian Martial Art Of Lancaster.

Steve Ijames	Major with Missouri PD, 29 year LEO; Original member of NTOA; former Chief Of Police
Stephen Satterly schoolsafetyshield@gmail.com Twitter: @StayAliveSteve	Co-Author of *Staying Alive: How to Act Fast and Survive Deadly Encounters*, School Safety Expert
Sudip Bose admin@thebattlecontinues.org	★ Recognized as one of the "**Leading Physicians of the World**" by the International Association of Healthcare Professionals ★ **Iraq war veteran**, recognized as a "**CNN Hero**" for receiving the **Bronze Star** and being selected as the US physician who **treated Saddam Hussein** after his capture. He served one of the longest continuous combat tours by a military physician since World War II ★ Founder of The Battle Continues Inc., a **nonprofit charity** serving injured veterans. We cover all administrative costs and

	100% of donations go to injured veterans. (www.TheBattleContinues.org) ★ International Public Speaker (www.SudipBoseSpeaker.com) ★ Chief Medical officer and Co-founder of liveClinic (www.liveClinic.com) ★ Founder of several leading online medical training/education programs (www.AceYourBoards.com) **★ Featured physician** on hit worldwide **reality TV** show **"Untold Stories of the ER", The Dr. Oz Show,** as well as many other media outlets.
Thomas Hietala hietala.thomas@gmail.com	Police Training Officer in Central Oregon with over 15 years of LE Experience.
Timothy La Sage http://timothylasage.com/	First Sergeant USMC (ret); Featured on History Channel's *Sniper: Deadliest Missions*

Tom Taylor ttaylor@gavindebecker.com	Senior Advisor Protective Strategies, Gavin de Becker & Associates
Tony Branch http://coachtonybranch.com/	United States Navy April 21st, 1980 to April 30th, 2000; Author of 2 books; retired from coaching AAU Girls basketball after 30 years with a career personal coaching record of 600 wins to 134 losses; Received national attention when shown on an episode of the ABC Network hit reality TV show, *Secret Millionaire*
Tony Scotti tonyscotti@msn.com https://isdacenter.org/	Founder of International Security Driver Association & Executive Vice President and Principal Management Consultant with Vehicle Dynamics Institute
Troy Vest	Career Coast Guard Officer, specialized in CN/CT work in Central and South America.

Ward Smith ward.smith@kcpd.org	Sergeant Ward Smith Kansas City Missouri Police Department. Firearms Training and Tactics Section.
William Aprill www.aprillriskconsulting.com william@aprillriskconsulting.com	20 years of experience across the continuum of mental health care, consultant in post-traumatic interventions and general mental health practice. Clinical interviewer of violent offenders. Former deputy sheriff and Special Deputy US Marshal. National presenter to civilian, law enforcement, and military audiences on violent criminality and defensive preparedness

More Books by This Author

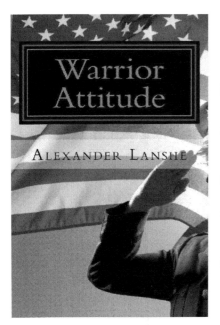

Warrior Attitude: 21 Ways to Think and Act Like a Warrior That Will Transform Your Outlook on Life.

"**One excellent book.**" - Lt. Col. Dave Grossman; Pulitzer Prize nominated author of *On Killing*, former Army Ranger and renowned expert on the psychology of killing

"**Congratulations on your book Warrior Attitude! You are a positive influence on youth and adults alike!**" - Julie Carrier; Former consultant to the Pentagon, best-selling author and nation's

#1 speaker for girls and young women, former Miss Virginia, featured on MTV's hit positive role model TV Show, *MADE*.

"The warrior mindset is truly the mindset of successful people. This book allows you to get your mindset corrected regardless of what stage you are at in life. I highly recommend this read for all." - Annie Carney; Former Executive Director of the LEAP Foundation, a leadership and life-development program for youth aged 15-24 on the campus of UCLA.

Warrior Attitude can be found on Amazon.com or go to www.AlexLanshe.com/books

Author Bio

Alexander Lanshe

National Speaker, Amazon #1

Best Selling Author and 20 year

veteran of martial arts, personal

protection, and combat fighting systems

Alexander Lanshe grew up in the greater Akron area in northeast Ohio with his parents and 6 younger siblings. He was homeschooled his entire life prior to going to the University of Akron where he received a Bachelor's of Science degree while double majoring in Exercise Science and Philosophy. Growing up, he held all manner of different jobs from Golf Caddy at the beautiful Donald Ross design of Congress Lake in Hartville, Ohio, to buss boy at the nation's largest dinner-theatre, to helping students succeed in academia, to working 1 day as a truck dispatcher.

From the age of 5 when his parents enrolled him in Karate, Alex has trained with and been mentored by some of the most influential protectors and warriors in the country. He has been teaching & training people just like you about martial arts, personal protection and self-defense for over a decade.

In 2014, Alex started his own company, Alexander Lanshe LLC, where he provides personal protection solutions to private individuals, groups, & companies. He has trained men and women from teacher's organizations, women's groups, university and college students, to current and former members of the military, including the US Navy, US Army Rangers and other branches.

In addition to the book you are reading, he is the Amazon-Published author of *Warrior Attitude: 21 Ways to Think and Act Like a Warrior that Will Transform Your Outlook on Life*, and co-author of the Amazon #1 Best Seller, *Rock Your Life: Encouraging Stories to Inspire and Motivate You to Rock Your Life*.

Alex's life mission is to protect other people from unjust violence by instilling in them the virtues of a warrior. He does this primarily through speaking engagements for small groups of a dozen to large conferences of thousands, writing guest articles and blogs, expanding his private client base, interviewing people on his podcast, *The Anatomy of a Warrior Show*, or by appearing as a guest on radio, TV or podcast interviews.

He is a national speaker, founder of www.AlexLanshe.com, and www.AnatomyOfaWarrior.com, blogger, serial interviewer, modern weaponry innovator, prefers dogs over cats, loves to play sand volleyball with his family, has been classically trained in Japanese Swordsmanship and once shared the stage with a vomiting Rudy Ruettiger, the man whose story inspired the blockbuster football film, "Rudy".

Follow the Author

Website	www.AlexLanshe.com
Email	Info@AlexLanshe.com
Facebook	https://www.facebook.com/anatomyofawarrior/
How to Book Alex to Speak	www.alexlanshe.com/speaking
Subscribe to *The Anatomy of a Warrior Show* YouTube Channel	https://www.youtube.com/channel/UCB4Y_6Rwcgg1t6k2X-ZqDlg
<u>Where to get more Books</u>: *Warrior Attitude: 21 Ways to Think and Act Like a Warrior That Will Transform Your Outlook on Life*	https://www.amazon.com/Warrior-Attitude-Think-Transform-Outlook/dp/1505654920/ref=sr_1_1?ie=UTF8&qid=1504373623&sr=8-1&keywords=warrior+attitude Or, search "Warrior Attitude" on Amazon.com

Become an exclusive supporter and patron of *The Anatomy of a Warrior Show* for access to exclusive, members-only podcasts, interviews, martial training videos, behind-the-scenes vlogs, blogs, book reviews, bonuses, and early access to content, surprises, and more!	https://www.patreon.com/aow
Donate to support the proliferation of the warrior virtues & the production of new content If you believe in the warrior virtues, donate and ask others to donate too!	PayPal link: https://www.paypal.me/AlexanderLansheLLC
Subscribe to *The Anatomy of a Warrior Show* free email list – visit the link and enter your name and email in the subscription box!	https://www.alexlanshe.com/

"As a physician studies disease to promote health, I study violence to promote peace." – Alexander Lanshe

"Sometimes the greatest love is not to sacrifice your life, but to live a life of sacrifice." Lt. Col. Dave Grossman

Made in the USA
San Bernardino, CA
18 October 2018